IT'S WORTH THE WAIT

LOVE | HOPE | STRENGTH

BASED ON A TRUE STORY

EVANS & PURIST OGBOI

Unless otherwise indicated, all scripture quotations are taken from the King James Version of the Holy Bible.

IT'S WORTH THE WAIT – LOVE, HOPE, STRENGTH

ISBN: 978-1-64370-984-0

Front Cover Design by McDonald Agbonifo
Published by WiMo Publications
www.wimopublishers.com
Printed in the United Kingdom

Acknowledgement

We give thanks to the Lord God Almighty for the salvation of our souls and for being such a Master Planner, the orchestrator of our life's journey... we worship you Lord. Thank You Jesus!

To our Parents, what can we say? We wouldn't be here today if it wasn't for your dogged determination to bring us up in the fear of God, putting us on the path of life… Thank you Dads – Pastor Jonathan Nduchukwuka and late Lawrence Ogboi! Thank you mums – Roseline Ogboi and Mabel Nduchukwuka – we could never repay your love!

To all our Siblings…. You all rock! This is *OUR STORY!!!* We love you guys strong!

To our spiritual parents – Pastor Chris and Abi Adeoye, Pastors of RCCG Living Faith Connections, London, UK. We thank you for your ceaseless prayers, encouragement and support within these beautiful years. You were there right from the inception of our marriage. Thank you for being the angels that you are. WE LOVE YOU STRONG!

To all our Friends, Family and Fans worldwide – those who prayed for us and have supported us over the years, God bless you all!

Dedication

For everyone waiting on the Lord for answered prayers…
The only thing that stands between you
and the fulfilment of your dreams is time.
If you can persevere, you will make it through,
and surely enter into your rest –
It's never over, till you win!

For Kairos

Forward

The Journey of Faithfulness

A testimony is a joyful experience and there are several ways folks use to express the manifestation of an expectation:

Finally!

At last!

Thank you Lord!

I stopped using the phrases "*I understand how you feel,*" or "*I know what you are going through,*" because the reality is: you can never really know how anyone feels. No matter how detailed an explanation is, you can never feel the pain or understand how much that person hurts.

When Evans and Purist asked that I write a forward to the book they had vowed to write to share their unique story, I felt honoured indeed. Without a doubt, their story is unique and I believe their testimony should be shared, to the Glory of God.

Getting married is blissful – the wedding excitement, the joy leading to the marriage, the laughter, the colourful wedding service, the beautiful outfits, the sumptuous wedding reception, the energetic dancing of the bride and groom, the mouth-watering delicacies served during the reception, the posing for photographs, the joy of in-laws and extended families, the honeymoon – and the list goes on.

After all of that, the couple starts their life together with great expectations, and I am sure that Evans and Purist had such dreams too, like every newly-wed is expected to.

This book is a true testimony of the fact that though weeping may endure all night, there is ALWAYS a morning that must release joy! This book is their testimony in words that God is truly, truly faithful. He never fails; O, God never fails!

I pray that this book doesn't just encourage you, but provokes you to wait on the Lord, just like David said in Psalm 27:13-14!

Christian Adeoye
Lead Pastor
RCCG Living Faith Connections,
London, UK.

Table of Contents

Section One:

Journey To God
1997 - 2005

1

Purist

1996. Lagos, Nigeria.

My heart was beating like a drum.

In the next room, I could hear Sister Foyin's voice modulating as she reported me to my parents. At the background, the lyrics of Cece Winans' *Alabastar Box* drifted, but my thoughts were far away.

Sister Foyin was a member of our church, a woman in her mid-thirties who was loud, and always trailing me with her watchful eyes as I went about church, or anywhere else she saw me. She had a sharp tongue, a suspicious eye, and she was quick to share her thoughts and observations to as many that cared to listen.

Today, my parents had become her sounding board, and as usual, she had filled their ears with the stories of everything that I had done.

Tears built in my eyes, I knew what was going to follow next.

"Purist!"

It was my father's gruff voice, and as I hastened to my feet and went to respond to his call, I wiped the first sign of tears.

By the time I got there, Sister Foyin was gone, but the bitter seeds she had sown with her words had taken her place. My father turned his angry eyes towards me.

"Did you hear what Sister Foyin said?"

I shook my head, but I had a pretty good idea. She would have ranted about how she saw me with a boy the previous day.

She would not have told them that the boy, Paul, was a member of the choir who had gotten into a big argument with his parents, and I had been trying to calm him down, and explain to him that he had to go back and apologise to them.

She wouldn't have told them, because she didn't know what had really happened. She just stumbled into us talking quietly in a corner, didn't ask me any questions, she drew up her false conclusions in her little mind, and looked for people to feed her lies with.

"It didn't happen like that," I tried to explain. "It's not what you think, Dad," but my father interrupted hastily, and he reeled out my punishment for the offence I had not even committed.

I never even got a chance to tell my side of the story.

It happened too often.

Why didn't they listen to me?

Growing up for me was not a rosy experience.

I had a rough time trying to meet the high expectations of my parents, the society, and church folk – and I also had five younger siblings who I had to be a *good example* to. It didn't make it any easier for me that my parents were pastors, and I belonged to the elite *Pastors Kids' Club.*

I had to be the perfect child, and it constantly put me under pressure. It was tough, but there was no easy way out.

In church, it was a whole new different game.

Sometimes I felt people like Sister Foyin hated me, and were always looking for something to point out to my parents, and say *look, the preacher's daughter made a mistake! The preacher's daughter is hanging around boys. How horrific, how hideous!*

I was always being reported to my parents.

I was punished many times, and I just wished they would listen to my side of the story. As long as the brother or sister that was speaking was older than I was, there was nothing I could say about this. No one ever listened to me.

School was not any different.

At school, I kept to myself most of the time and walked in the shadow of the other kids.

I was no *queen-bee*, I had no friends flocking around me, or people wanting my attention. I was at best, invisible to the world, and everyone else around me.

I wore braces and large round glasses, and I walked around with books clutched tightly in my hand, with my head characteristically hanging downwards. None of the kids would want to hang around me, not when there were other girls with flashing confident smiles, tall and slender gaits, and fair beautiful skin.

A girl walked past me. She looked like a nice sort. I peeked at her through my glasses, and I smiled, exposing my braces – she looked right through me. She didn't smile back.

My head shot back down. Most of the time I walked around with my head down, looking at my shoes, I could not bear to look at anyone. I hardly looked people in the eye, and there was nothing to say, or I never seemed to find the right words.

I tried so hard to fit in, I tried to fit into several groups. I didn't have friends, and every time I tried to make friends, I was met with a brick wall.

The other girls were always mean.

I was always misunderstood.

The friendships I had never quite panned out the way I wanted. They always ended on a sour note, with me either way, getting hurt. It pushed me even farther away from people.

Why am I so different? Why am I different from everyone else?

I asked myself this question for the hundredth time as I walked to my classroom. No one seemed to understand me. In the middle of all the discordant thoughts, music found me.

In my heart, I could hear music play. Music gave me a hiding place and safe haven from the barrage of the world. It gave me the comfort I needed from the demanding role of being the perfect preacher's kid at home, and the isolated geeky girl in school.

2

Evans

1996. Benin City, Nigeria.

"Wake up!"

It was 6am. I had been having the best dream ever when I heard the tap on my back.

I was drowsy, and the night had not been long enough.

"Morning devotion…"

I dragged myself out of bed, along with my siblings. Armed with our bibles, and with groggy eyes, we trooped to the living room, the venue for our morning devotion.

I heard the giggles, I knew something was wrong, but I couldn't resist closing my eyes again. I yawned. I had not gotten enough sleep. I just wished I could dive back into my bed.

"Evans, stand up!" the giggles were even louder.

I turned, and my father was looking at me directly. I realised my siblings had been trying to get my attention in the first place; and they had been trying to warn me that my father had caught me dozing.

"Read 1 Kings 1…" My father instructed.

My hand moved swiftly over the pages of the bible, and as I rested on the portion to be read, my eyes turned to my father, in disbelief. "There are fifty three verses," I said in light protest. *Fifty three long, boring verses – did we really have to read the whole chapter? It was 6.04am! Geez!*

"I know," he began. "Read everything."

More giggles. I began to read, I was struggling to keep awake and read at the same time. Somewhere along the line, the words of King James became blurred, my speech muffled, I lost my train of thought. I must have fallen asleep again.

"Evans!" Amidst my siblings' quiet laughter and stifled giggles, my dad's stern voice brought me back from my reverie. "Start from the beginning!"

Such was the typical home in which I grew up.

My growing up was fun! I was born into a Christian family of six, and my mum and dad were both members of Deeper Life Bible Church at the time.

Mornings were characteristically filled with devotion, prayer, and study of the bible. It was a time we had come to love and dread. It was sometimes boring, and other times, we found ways to make it as entertaining as we could.

Those days shaped my life.

Growing up was a roller coaster experience. At about the time I was born, there was plenty. My parents were well off, my father was working with Nigerian Airways at the time, we travelled by air, went on holidays, and then and all of a sudden, things changed drastically.

From living in affluence, poverty suddenly hit – my father lost everything, and things got very bad. I remember there was a point we were evicted from the house we lived because we couldn't afford to pay the rent.

There were days our parents would stay up worried about where we would get money to buy the next meal, or pay the bills, and provide good clothing. There were days we couldn't go to school because we couldn't afford to pay for tuition.

Generally, it was fun growing up, but the see-saw experiences of watching my parents struggle at some points was not always pleasurable.

My parents went to church regularly, and as I tagged along with them, my passion for God began to rise.

1997. Benin City, Nigeria.

The music was deafening.

Cigarette wisps circled the young men, who stood with sagging trousers, and slanting stances, speaking slangs, and acting *cool*. I stood at a distance, and watched with longing in my eyes. I wanted to be part of this group.

I can really do this…I want to live this life.

Internal challenges began during my early youthful years, peer pressure heightened especially at the time I was about to finish high school. There was the growing pressure to join gangs, fit in with the *boys,* hang out with girls, and *cultism* was the in-thing.

I had friends who were aspiring to belong to fraternities. The fraternities in Nigerian campuses were a refined version of gangster-clubs where violence reigned, and members were involved in vices, expensive living, and regular deadly clashes with other fraternities. Despite the seeming danger such clubs portrayed, it was common lingua for young guys to say: "*When I get into college, I will join this fraternity, which one are you joining?*"

I planned to have a full taste of this sort of life. I didn't smoke, didn't drink, but I craved for the life and the excitement that the fast lane offered. I was standing outside, looking in. I had been brought up by my father to *love what was righteous, and eschew evil*, but a part of me wanted this fast-paced, gangster-typed life – I wanted to belong to this other world.

I had grown up in a Christian family, I regularly attended church, but I was also in that thing called *school*. I wasn't attending church in school; I was going to school, and school came with all sorts of things – pressure to belong, and to be accepted and celebrated when you were perceived as belonging to the *in-clique.*

Like every other teenage boy, I really wanted to belong, and to fit into that *in-clique.* Many times, I was tempted to compromise... I *wanted* to compromise. The word of God, and morning devotion seemed so far away when you were contending with becoming part of the *happening guys* in high school.

There was a call upon my life, and I didn't even know it. It was the reason why although I tried to blend into the world of the *big bad boys*, I couldn't fit in. The pressure to conform to bad influence was strong, but as much as I tried, it never worked out.

I was looking so foolish, and the harder I tried to get into that way of life, God was working twice as hard to pull me out of it.

I looked again at the boys within the crowd, they had stolen away from their homes to smoke, drink and do other things that made them feel stronger than everyone else.

Evans, what are you doing here?

A voice asked within me.

You don't belong here.

I knew it, the boys knew it, and God knew it too.

I walked away from that little crowd, feeling rather silly. I couldn't do these things. As much as I tried, there was something in me that was totally repulsed to it. But I wanted to be around it – it was a mix of contradictions.

There's no point trying to fit into a place where I wasn't wanted, I slowly decided.

I began to hum as I walked home. I felt the music stirring within me.

The minute I turned away and decided I wasn't going to spend my life living in vices, the next best thing was music.

I fell hard, and I fell fast.

Music consumed me, and it became my passion – my waking and sleeping thought. Music was my escape in my youthful days from the bad gangs, and all the things that were done in school that I couldn't fit into.

With my school bag on my back, after school had closed for the day, I left school but instead of heading home like had become my usual routine, I turned into a building at the corner of Ekenwan

Road. In front of it, a signboard stood high: *Church of God Mission*. It was one of the many parishes of a popular Pentecostal Church in Benin City, Nigeria.

As I got in, the church was quiet, no one was there, and I dropped my school bag and went to get out the drums.

The five-piece drum set looked so lonely, sitting there on its own. Alone with the drums, here was my chance to do something.

I assembled the drums, but I didn't have a clue how to begin. I sat behind the drums, lifted the drum sticks, and I tried to imitate what I had seen skilful drummers do. I began to play with as much passion as I could muster.

I must have been making a lot of discordant noise, but I put my heart and soul into it. I believed that if I practiced harder, someday I would sound like I was actually drumming.

I heard a sound, and I looked up. It was the resident pastor, who had probably come to enquire who was creating the disturbance. When he saw me, his eyes paused briefly, and for a second, I thought he would ask me to leave. He just looked at me with a stiff smile, gave a brief nod, and walked back into his office.

He probably guessed I needed the drums more than the drums needed me.

Those days I spent alone with the drums in that church auditorium along Ekenwan Road marked the beginning of my passion and love for music and all things musical.

My love for music started slowly, and then erupted into a gushing spring, moving fast to other things. I mastered the art of playing the drums, and I began to play the keyboard, and soon I heard a church needed someone to play for them. I offered my services and I developed my skills, in the process.

I also started to teach songs to the choir, and at a time, I was leading my teenage choir. Then I began to write songs, and I started to create my own beats! I discovered a whole new world that intoxicated me, and I was consumed with the entirety of music.

My peers were crazy about girls, embroiled in one vice or another – I had my music. It meant everything to me, and replaced the need to succumb to peer-pressure. Music pressured me enough, and filled my thoughts all day.

I would take the church keyboard home and try to program beats, and sometimes I would go for a whole day and sometimes, nights, without eating anything, just making music.

Music was as such a strong passion that after Sunday service, the first thing I thought was "*Wow, the next choir rehearsal is on Thursday – how am I going to survive until then?*"

I remember my mother got upset with me once, and as I was about to leave for choir rehearsal, she refused and said I wasn't going. She usually threatened to stop me from attending choir rehearsal, but eventually she'd let me off. This time it was different.

I could see it in her eyes. She meant her words. I was not leaving the house.

"I don't even know if that's where you're *really* going," she began. "You always say you're going for choir rehearsal, *choir rehearsal* – which kind of rehearsal is that?"

Truth be told, she probably thought choir rehearsal was my excuse for getting out of the house, and disappearing for hours. She might have imagined I was involved in vices, or bad habits, and she couldn't understand how a teenage boy would be so consumed with music the way I had been.

"You're not leaving this house today," she said firmly, her eyes not leaving mine.

Time literally stopped, and my heart froze as the reality dawned on me. I wasn't going to attend choir rehearsal that day. "Mummy, please," the tears started rolling down before I realised it. "Mummy please, I am sorry, I'll do anything, but please let me go for my rehearsal."

She was shocked. I hardly cried, if ever, and it began to dawn on her that music for me was very important, bordering on the line of an obsession, and it was something I had taken quite seriously too, even though I was young.

My mother reluctantly allowed me attend the rehearsal that day, but she also went ahead to meet the choir leader, and enquire from him if I had been attending rehearsals, and his response shocked her.

"Oh yes, Brother Evans is the most committed member of this choir," he told her with pride. "He comes before we start, he arranges the chairs, and he's always the last to leave – he's a dedicated young lad, and he's really passionate about the choir."

From that day, I sensed my mother's relief that I was not involved with any vices, and her respect for me and my love for music grew. My mother never threatened to stop me from attending choir rehearsal again, and instead, she found ways she could be of support. She released me to my passion, made excuses for me to help me focus on my music, and with her unspoken support for my new found talent, my skill began to grow.

3

Purist

1997. Lagos, Nigeria

This could not be happening to me.

I felt like choking.

I was always being misunderstood. Life was really tough.

No one likes me.

I'm not pretty enough.

I'm not good enough.

The thoughts raged within my heart, and as I sat in the dark alone, thoughts ran wild in my head. Like a thief in the night, a flood of negative thoughts swept into my heart, made a comfortable home in it, and from there, began to grow and fester.

I was fifteen, but I felt I carried the burden of a fifty year old.

Pressure in my life was a constant feature. I wished I had a fun-filled life like some of the girls I saw in school. They looked like their lives were big endless parties, and my life seemed so difficult; it all seemed so unfair!

Why does everyone expect me to be perfect? It's not fair!

My self-confidence began to wane.

I can't deal with anyone anymore, this is too much, I just can't take it anymore.

Finding a way out seemed like a good idea.

I had made up my mind. Today was the day I would end my life, today was the day that I solved all my problems.

In one my hand, I held an open jar of paracetamol, and in the other was a chunk of pills. I was not thinking of anything else but ending this and dulling my pain forever.

I began to swallow the tablets. I was not thinking, I just wanted to get rid of the pain, I wanted to end my sorrow and my anguish – and I was taking the easy way out.

Why are you doing this? Remember what Jesus did for you on the cross of

Calvary.

At that point I realised how foolish that decision had been and there and then, I got on my knees and asked Jesus into my life. My hands were clasped together, as I asked Jesus to forgive me and become my Saviour.

I had been in church for so long, I had heard the salvation prayers for even longer, but I had never said them myself.

This was a personal decision, one I took without a preacher prompting me or my parents mandating me, it was a choice I made when I realised I could no longer hold my life together by myself.

Lord Jesus, I need you…

Lord Jesus, I come to you now… I acknowledge that I am a sinner… I believe that you died for me… Please accept me… wash me with Your blood.
Please come into my life…
Redeem me…

I felt His loving arms wrap around me. I knew this was the best decision I would ever make in my life.

I haven't looked back ever since.

Evans

2000. Benin City, Nigeria.

It was the first day of the year.

It was year 2000 - the new millennium.

Everyone had looked forward to the new millennium with uncertainty and trepidation.

There had been panic everywhere.

Many believed the world was coming to an end, computers would crash, and the world as we knew it would cease to exist.

My world, like everyone else's was thrown into confusion.

On the last day of the year, people flooded churches, with the fear that the world was coming to an end.

I was one of them. I was always in church, but I didn't have much of a relationship with God. I was scared to the bone, and my eyes always went to the gigantic clock that stood at the centre of the main entrance into the church.

True I loved the music, and it was gospel, but that was where it stopped.

I didn't know God, not the way some of the people in church did. They would talk about God like He was a person, someone they knew – a friend. During worship, they would lift their hands to heaven, and a stream of tears would flow down their eyes. I was a musician, I created the music, but I didn't have that. And I desired it, I wanted it.

The 31st day of December, 1999 was the longest night ever. And when the clock struck 12, and nothing happened, amidst the shouts of happy New Year, I struggled to regain my composure.

Is this it? Are we still here?

The world hadn't ended.

The sky had not fallen in either.

There were no computers crashing, or clocks spiralling out of control. Everywhere was relatively calm and peaceful, nothing like what I had been expecting.

My feet were still shaking when I got home. I had been frightened that the world was going to end, that Jesus was coming to take His people home, and then I would be nowhere to be found.

The thought of that made me feel so empty. What if indeed, He had come – what would have become of me? I suddenly felt a hollow in my heart.

Lord, Jesus I need you…

Somehow, I felt myself reaching for God from within. There was a void that needed to be filled. I had been in church for years, but the void was still there.

For three years, I had been playing music in church, and had taken it up as a job. I was the official drummer of my church.

I had music, but it still was not enough. There were places even the most crafted notes could not touch, and there were certain valleys in my heart that even music couldn't fill.

I have music, but it's not enough...

I never wanted to experience this hopelessness again.

Lord, I don't want to be unserious anymore...

I fell on my knees and pledged my life, my heart and my desires to God. I asked for His help to live a Christian life, and I pledged to take my Christian walk with all seriousness, hence forth.

That day, my life changed, and I purposefully started my journey of faith.

4

Evans

2003. Lagos, Nigeria.

I decided to leave Benin City and move to the city of Lagos. I left my family, like God told Abraham to leave his father's house. I left Benin City for Lagos to pursue my music and work with a church.

It was three years after I had made that decision to walk with God. I had finished high school, and plans where underway for me to attend college.

My father wanted me to be an accountant, and I might have had the skills, and the grades, but I really wanted to study a course in music or something music-related, but I was still not very clear what direction to take.

When I decided to go to Lagos, my parents did not stand in my way, but gave as much support as I required.

Moving to Lagos was a faith-walk, it was an adventure, and I was determined that God would take me by the hand and lead me where He wanted me to go.

I was living in Anthony Village, a little town in the heart of the mainland in Lagos, Nigeria. There was an RCCG parish right on my street, and I felt a leading from the Lord to go there and pray, every day.

I heeded the prompt, and I would go to that church every day, and just spend time communing with God. By spending time with God, my spiritual life began to grow.

I was learning to trust God, walk with God, and cultivate my prayer life, and as a result, I saw God move in so many ways in my life. I started getting the nudge to preach in commercial buses during my regular commute, and I had a strong prompt to share the gospel of Christ with people I met each day.

Each time I thought of preaching in a bus, a scripture my elder brother Harry regularly quoted would ring warning bells in my head.

Tarry in Jerusalem until you're endued with power.

Harry had strong faith, he was a prayer warrior, and this was one of the several scriptures he was fond of quoting. Although I hadn't seen him in recent times, I wondered why it kept ringing in my head.

I walked up to my pastor a few days later, and told him I had a strong burden to preach, but I always felt a withdrawal, and told him about the scripture that kept replaying in my heart.

"Do I need to be *endued with power* before I can preach?" I asked him.

"Well, not really, but you would be much more effective if you are," he responded. "Do you want to be filled with the Holy Ghost?" he asked me.

I nodded. If being filled with the Holy Ghost would make me preach effectively, yes, I did.

He took me by the hand, and prayed with me. I was immediately filled with the Holy Spirit, and I began to speak in tongues from that day.

Oh, what joy I felt!

I left the church for my house, and within my spirit, I felt it, I could almost touch the overflow – I was filled!

As I boarded a bus and sat at the back of the bus, excitement bubbled from within me. I began to preach the word even before the bus departed. I preached with so much relish and fervour, passengers kept looking behind – wondering who was speaking.

When I got home, I fell on my knees, and I couldn't stop praying in the Holy Ghost – I was so excited. My life with God took a quantum leap from that day forward.

2004. Lagos, Nigeria.

I stumbled on a book written by Myles Munroe – *In Pursuit of Purpose.* By this time, I had begun to develop my relationship with the Holy Spirit, and I could hear Him speak to me. I knew within me that I was meant to read this book – everything about it drew me to it, and I bought it and took it home.

It took me a couple of days to begin reading the book, but when I finally started, I was hooked from the first page.

Every line, every phrase, felt as if it had been written specially for me, and had been packaged and sent to me, all the way from the little Caribbean island of the Bahamas.

Up until that point, I had never thought about certain things, but in that book, Myles Munroe shared certain principles that literally blew my mind.

Your gifts are clues to your purpose.

I began to ask the question more importantly – *what's my purpose in life?*

The question taunted me, it nudged in my spirit. I had a hunch, and a direction, but I needed to be sure. I didn't want to gamble with one of the most important decisions of my life.

I took out three days to wait upon the Lord, and during this time, I prayed, I studied the word of God, I worshipped and I meditated. By the end of the three day duration, I knew what I had to do.

I travelled to Benin to see my parents and let them know that I had taken a major life decision – I was going to go into the music ministry, full time.

I expected my father to have an argument, or put up a resistance. It had always been his dream for me to be an accountant, and I was not sure if he would like this idea of me becoming a musician.

As I spoke with him that day, determination set in my eyes, I was surprised by his response.

"If you have to do music, then do it professionally, to the highest standard possible," was his summation. "Travel to London, and find a school where you can study music."

I had intentions of studying abroad but I had never shared them with my father. He had spoken like a prophet, and his agreement and support had been a major confirmation that I was on the right track. It was indeed God's will that music became my career.

With my parents' blessings and full support, I returned to Lagos feeling energized and ready to take on the world! I tried to get enrolled in *Berkley College of Music* in America, but that didn't work out.

I shared my passion with someone in my church, and he paid for me to attend a production course at *Eko Reel Mix Studios*, which at the time was one of the biggest studios in West Africa.

I learned as much as I could about music production and audio engineering, and in little to no time, I had carved quite a niche for myself.

I set up a home studio, and there were a good number of young talents and musicians lining up, to work with me. It was exciting.

It was on this journey that I met my wife.

Purist

1999. Lagos, Nigeria.

My hand clutched the microphone as I sang, my heart lifted, my voice ringing.

I found joy in church. It was my safe haven and I always looked forward to choir practice.

Church felt like an escape from all the demands that had been placed on me and it was the best place to be for me. Coupled with my love for music that slowly turned to an addiction, I was always drawn to the church, it felt like home.

I found consolation every time I sang. It seemed a vault opened up every time I lifted my voice to heaven and belted out notes.

My parents were a huge part of the discovery of my passion for music – they led me to church at a young age, and because I was in church, I discovered the beauty of music pretty quickly, and always found myself singing.

We were members of the Deeper Life Bible Church, and I joined the church choir at a very tender age. Even though everyone looked at me funny whenever I sang – I sang with so much passion and zest, despite being so young – I never stopped!

I was such a die-hard fan of music, I loved singing, enjoyed every bit of it, I was passionate about it.

My Dad went on to start his own ministry and as all new churches start out, the Pastor's kids got to do *everything – I* was in the choir, I played the keyboard, my siblings and I set up the sound system for every service in church, and for a number of years, I directed the choir. This drove my passion for music deeper and gave me some sort of confidence in the gift of singing that God had placed in me.

2000. Benin City, Nigeria.

As a young believer, I spent so much time studying the bible, praying and serving in God's house.

I soon became an undergraduate at the University of Benin, and joined The Redeemed Christian Fellowship (RCF), a campus fellowship outreach of the Redeemed Christian Church of God. There, I found an opportunity to serve, and grow in my walk with God.

I was crazy for God! I'd go for choir practice, bible study, church meetings, and retreats. I found joy studying the scriptures, praying, and singing. I had a strong passion to serve God, and sometimes I would skip classes because I needed to be at church or do something for my fellowship.

Doing these things for God just gave me peace. I served with my heart, not unto man, but unto God.

I enjoyed serving God! Doing things for God, serving at the church was never a burden, and was never stressful. It didn't matter the task, I just dived in with excitement and a drive to deliver results!

I never missed any church activity and I held those days of active service at the campus fellowship so dear to my heart.

There was so much to look forward to, many cherished moments, beautiful experiences I had in the presence of God.

My walk with God kept unfolding each day, and I kept growing and attaining more beautiful heights, and remarkable depths.

5

Evans & Purist

In so many ways, there are people who are looking for a connection with God.

Looking back now, the most important thing is to fear God and keep His commandments. There is no dream, aspiration, absolutely nothing that is greater than God – God is in charge of everything.

To the young person reading this, we will encourage you to serve the Lord in the days of your youth, just like we did. The more foundation of God you have in your life, the better it will be for your future.

The Scriptures say in Psalm 11:3: *If the foundation be destroyed, what can the righteous do?*

It is important to get the foundation of your life right. If your foundation is invested in God, He will take care of you.

Connecting With God

Your connection with God is all about your daily communication with God. There are two keys that have worked for us: the study of the word and praying in the Holy Ghost. The word of God and prayer is very important – these are the things we grew up with.

Jesus said, *man shall not live by bread alone, but by every word that that proceedeth out of the mouth of God (Matt4:4).* When you have not read the bible, you should feel starved, as the study of the word is integral to a thriving Christian walk with God.

Prayer is not trying to impress with a lot of *christianese*, it is an awesome opportunity to talk to a great God, that Jesus has afforded us in His name.

Pray in the Holy Ghost, begin each day with worship and commit each day into His hands, and in the evening, kneel before God and thank Him for the day.

Prayer, worship and the Word of God – are strong keys, these are tools for living out your faith, especially praying in the Holy Ghost. It's so potent, that its effect on an individual's life cannot be explained.

Listen to messages and teachings by seasoned men of God. Learn about faith, love, and activate your faith.

Read Christian material, worship and fellowship with other believers; this will grow your faith, and your walk with God significantly.

Giving Your Lifetime To Jesus

From the moment we decided to give God our lifetime, it has been a journey that we have not regretted. If you decide to give God your lifetime, like we did, He will take care of you, and He will never let you down.

To someone that needs to find God, believe that God exists.

The bible teaches that God *is a rewarder of them that diligently seek Him (Hebrews11:6)*. Faith is *believing*. You can't see him, but you know he exists – that's what faith is.

He knows *your* name.

He sent Jesus to die for *you.*

Whosoever believes in Him will not perish.

The first step is to believe.

You have to confess Jesus Christ as the Lord of your life, just like we did.

After you have done this, find a bible believing Church, get nurtured by a strong, sound pastor, get around sound believers and get in the bible.

First believe and confess that Jesus is Lord, and then get around people that will influence you positively.

Get into spiritual activities, start to read the word, start to find God yourself, desire the infilling and baptism of the Holy Spirit, begin to speak in tongues. Pray for one hour every day, proceed to three hours, and grow from strength to strength, and then you will see God taking you to realms you never imagined you would get to.

Fighting Temptations

Having a beautiful walk with God and communion and fellowship with Him is amazing, but you can't remain in church all the time. Every time we had to get into the *real world,* we had temptations staring us in the face.

In your Christian walk, it is one thing to receive the power from God, and to have a great relationship with God. It's another thing to walk according to God's word.

As young people, we faced the same challenges other young people faced – pornography, lust, vanity, pride – it was everywhere we turned. We cried to God for strength, and sought for the grace to live above these things. We began to learn to ask the Lord for help.

The scripture says in Psalm 119 verse 9: ***How can the youth cleanse their way except the word. Thy word have I hid in my heart.***

And we began to hold unto God's word, and walk with God, we received His grace. Living above sin was not easy, it was a daily walk, it was a battle, but by letting the Holy Spirit take charge, we recorded victory.

You too can walk in victory. You too can fight, and stand for God – firm and strong!

Section Two:

Journey To Marriage
2006 - 2012

6

Evans

2006. Lagos, Nigeria.

As a youth growing up, two of my biggest misconceptions about marriage were that marriage is very complicated and tough and that I needed to have everything – a big house, a good car, and a well-paying job before I even started to think about marriage.

Most of the older married people around me made me think I had to be super financially prepared before making the *big decision*.

And they succeeded.

I totally bought into it – *to be married, you have to be super-rich, and financially loaded* – it was all I heard. And so I believed it.

My mind had been conditioned to think I had to wait until I had it all planned and arranged, I was about to find out that God worked differently.

I had always known that the first thing I wanted in a wife was someone who had the fear of God and for some reason, I was certain I was going to end up with a *Preacher's Kid,* which eventually happened!

I prayed about this because I knew that having a spouse who had the fear of God and wanted to please God was the only way a marriage was going to work. Once we both were obeying God, the marriage was sure to thrive and succeed.

The second quality I was looking out for was a woman who could sing. I desired strongly to have a singer as a wife; I wanted someone who could work with me in my music ministry.

The third quality I looked for was a woman who was ready to join me in full time music ministry. I didn't want to be married to someone who worked in a different industry and didn't understand the lifestyle of a music minister. I didn't want a situation where I would have to travel a lot and leave my *banker* or *lawyer wife* at home.

This was so important to me because full time ministry was my life goal and I needed a wife who not only understood this, but was willing to join me on that journey. I wanted somebody who was humble, someone who was meek and obviously pretty.

I had a few singer friends at the time who I'd met in church, but none of them was *the will of God*, to the best of my knowledge.

And then I met Purist.

Purist

2006. Lagos, Nigeria

I read a lot of novels when growing up, and it influenced and created a picture in my head of who I would like to get married to. The novels created a picture in my head – the man of my dreams had to be fine, handsome, outgoing and protective. Those were things that growing up shaped my thinking about who I would get married to.

As I grew older, I became more mature in my thinking, and my dad became one of the models of an ideal husband for me. I loved the way he treated my mother, the way he protected her from in-laws, and the way he respected her, and I wanted to marry someone like my dad, someone that would do the same for me.

My father had always encouraged my siblings and I to pray for our life partners.

The first time I heard him say it, it didn't make any sense, but somehow, it became a part of me.

I spent a good chunk of my time as a young believer praying for my future husband.

I prayed for his covering.

I prayed that he would be a man after God's own heart.

I prayed the he would be a man who will protect and love me for who I am.

I prayed that he would be a man with a sweet, meek and gentle spirit.

I had always had my fair share of young men coming around, but I had not settled in my spirit that any of them was the one for me.

When I met Evans, the last thing I was looking to find was a husband.

I wanted to release a single, and I had worked with a couple of producers on the project, but I had not found what I was looking for. I had a good ear for music. I heard sounds in my head, and I knew exactly how I wanted my music to sound, but none of the producers I had worked with were interpreting the music the way I felt it. It was all wrong!

Frustrated and confused, I was in Lagos, back on holidays from school and I went to see Segun, a friend of mine who lived on the same street as I did.

Segun served at RICC Rehoboth international Christian centre, a church that sprung out of the Fountain of Life Church, and he was musically sound, and so I knew he would understand my predicament.

“I'm trying to work on a track,” I explained to Segun, “but the guys I'm trying to work with are just frustrating me!”

“Hey, it's okay,” he consoled, and then his eyes lit up suddenly. “Hey, why don't I introduce you to my music director in my church? He's really good, and I think he can deliver exactly what you're looking for.”

I was not so certain, as I had met other producers that had been dubbed *really good,* and I had still come away from the experience feeling dissatisfied. Segun persuaded me that his music director was different; he gave me his number and asked me to call him. “His name is Evans,” he told me.

I actually forgot about 'music director Evans' for a while until it was almost time to return to school. I finally called Evans, introduced myself and told him what I wanted to do.

He sounded like a nice, jolly fellow. Maybe he was the person that would finally turn the music in my head into the song I wanted to hear.

Evans

2006. Benin City, Nigeria.

My phone rang sometime in December of 2006.

I remember I was out of Lagos then, visiting with family in Benin.

"Hello," I answered the call, and it was a lady with a strong, confident voice at the other end.

"My name is Purist," she began. "Is this Evans?"

"Yes," I replied. *Purist*. I mused over the name. Was that her real name?

"I got your number from a friend, Segun," she continued.

"Oh, okay," I responded, as a mental picture of Segun, the base guitarist at the church where I also, fluttered into my mind.

"I'm looking for a producer for my song," she began. "He told me you're good at what you do, how can we meet?"

"Okay, Purist, I'm currently out of Lagos," I informed her, "Is that your real name though? Like your parents gave you the name *Purist*?"

I felt her stiffen at the other end, and then with a curt voice, "yes, that's my real name."

"Okay, Purist, like I said, I'm currently out of Lagos, but we can meet next year, probably in January, when I return."

She was in agreement, and we ended the conversation on that note.

Purist – an interesting name, with an interesting voice, I thought.

I went back to my holidaying, and thought nothing more of it.

7

Purist

2007. Lagos, Nigeria.

I stood in front of a car, I was wearing a pair of dark sunglasses, and I scanned around the crowd.

I was waiting to meet with Evans.

I had called him late last year, and after series of calls, we had finally decided on a place to meet.

He had chosen *Master Chef*, a fast-food joint close to the annex campus of Lagos State University in Anthony Village. I wasn't so sure if it had been a great choice. The place was thronging with rowdy, energetic students, and there was so much noise, it could have passed for a busy Lagos market.

I saw someone that stood out, and something told me this was the person I had come to meet. He was rather good looking, and just a bit taller than I was.

He caught my eye, and held my gaze. He was holding a phone. I rang him and he picked it up on the first ring, all the while looking right at me. How had he guessed I was the one?

We walked into the restaurant together, and sat down in one of the comfortable chairs.

The first few minutes were terse, I settled into a far corner, and took off my sunglasses.

"Can I get you a drink?" he asked me.

"Yes please, a bottle of sprite is fine," I said.

He darted over to the counter, and returned with a cold bottle of sprite and a straw. *He was such a gentleman.* He settled into the opposite side of the two-seater and we got talking.

We talked about my expectations for my song, and I shared some of my frustrations with the previous producers I had worked with. From there, we began to talk about other things – growing up, church, music, and I realised we had quite a lot in common.

And then, in the midst of our conversation, for the first time in my life, I heard God speak to me clearly:

This is the person you've been praying for... the one you've been waiting for.

I almost choked on my drink. I started to cough – *is this a joke?*

Evans looked at me with concerned eyes. "Are you alright?"

"I'm fine," I replied, looking back.

My husband? This was the last thing on my mind. Guys were all over me, a guy in the US who had even promised to get me a producer, and had actually proposed to me but I had ruled him out because I knew he was not God's plan for me and at the time, getting into a relationship was the last thing on my mind.

My eyes fell on Evans once more, and I felt unsettled when I thought of the words that had just dropped in my spirit.

All through the remainder of our meeting, my thoughts strayed far and wide, but no matter how much I tried to rationalise it, it just didn't make any sense.

This is a total stranger. You don't even know him.

Evans

2007. Lagos, Nigeria

I was scheduled to meet Purist and I walked quickly to the location I had chosen for our meet-up.

My house wasn't exactly great looking at the time, I lived in a small room, and that's where I also had my home studio, and so I usually preferred to meet prospective clients at any other location than my house.

I got to the restaurant where we had agreed to meet, I saw Purist and in less than a minute after we sat down, I heard in my spirit these exact words: *Do you know this could actually be your wife?*

This was the first time in my life and my walk with God that anything like this had happened. I had never heard God speak into my heart the way He did.

In that first meeting I learned so much about her, and as she told me about herself, the more convinced I was that she was *the one.*

When I met Purist, it's hard to explain all the things I saw in her; she was humble, cheerful and meek. She had such a meek spirit, an open and receptive heart.

I had met a lot of ladies before her, but she was unique, different, she was so open in her spirit. And I totally believe it was because she was the one meant for me. We had that immediate *click.*

There were just so many confirmations: she was into music, her dad was a pastor, she was so passionate about music, and she was talking about her passion, her family. In just a few minutes after we sat down to talk, we found out so many things about each other.

"I'm not usually like this," she said finally. "I don't really talk this much to a stranger..."

I went on to find out that our birth dates were just three days apart, but I was a year older than she was - a year and three days older. I found out she had applied to go to a particular music college, *Berklee College of Music* in Boston, the same I had also applied for, and that she was also as passionate about music as I was! It all just made perfect sense.

After our conversation, I took her to my home studio to show her some of the work I had done.

"After she comes here, will she come back?" Was the thought that kept ringing in my head, considering the state of my studio at the time.

I couldn't stop thinking about the voice I heard in my spirit, the way there were so many coincidences about both of us – could it be possible that I meet someone on the first day and know for certain that she was *the one*?

Later that evening, she was long gone, but I still couldn't shake off what had happened earlier, and I decided to share it with my friend Bernard, and seek counsel.

"Bernard," I called out to my friend, he was a strong Christian, and we had shared some great times together. "The strangest thing happened to me today," I told him.

"What happened?" curious, he turned to me.

I proceeded to tell him about my meeting with Purist – how I had heard in my spirit that she could be my wife, and how we just seemed to have *clicked* from the first conversation. I was not sure what I was to do next.

Bernard didn't sound particularly convinced. "Hey Evans, you just met her, and you never know," he began. He advised that I focus on my career, and on the job I was doing for her. "And well, if it's God's will, we'd find out in due time," he concluded.

Bernard's words made perfect sense at the time. So I kept my thoughts to myself, and I tried to push it far from my mind as much as I could.

8

Purist

2007. Lagos, Nigeria.

I went home, and I spoke to my siblings about my meeting with Evans, and what God had spoken to me, then I kept it in my mouth and heart, and Evans and I started on the project, talking on the phone.

First we talked only about the project, how it was going, and updates that needed to be sent in. After a while, we began to talk about other things beyond the project because we discovered that we had a lot of similarities.

With MTN *Extra Cool*, a telephone service bundle that allowed callers to have free calls from midnight to five am, we could speak for a long time, for free.

I realised my happiness for the day depended on hearing Evan's voice, and he didn't help matters – he always wanted to talk to me all the time, and give me updates on the progress he had made. We had become really good friends at this time, but I kept my feelings to myself.

What am I doing? I am falling for this guy.

When the realisation dawned, I tried to break it off, but Evans was handling the project and doing an amazing job with it.

For the first time, I met a producer who totally understood me. Sometimes it felt like we were plugged into the same musical space – he got me totally, he heard the notes I heard, and he used his skill to bring it to a reality.

We were immersed in the project together, getting the right chords, the right sequence, the right intro to the song. We did a lot of work through telephone conversations, and even when I had to go back to school, we continued talking, and the project advanced.

All through the period, I always sensed God's peace and in quiet solitude, I always remembered what God had spoken on the first day we met.

I decided I wasn't going to struggle. I would just hold on, follow God's leading, trust, and see how it all played out.

Evans

2007, Lagos, Nigeria

Over the next couple of months, I worked with Purist on her first song, My *Side of Story*, and it was just magical. The heavens were opened, and till date it's still the most powerful song I've done. The kind of inspiration I received was amazing!

Over time Purist and I became friends, we talked at length, shared challenges that we were currently having, and grew really close.

Purist was such a wonderful person; she spoke with such humility and brought sunshine along wherever she went. It was obvious that God had made her just for me. I had never met anyone like her, I always marvelled at how easily it was for me to connect with her, it was as though we had known each other for years. The click was immediate, the connection was strong.

She was teachable, patient, kind, in fact, she had all the fruits of the spirit and she was not faking it or trying to put up a façade. She had a great deal of self-confidence. And although she had some guards put up due to past experiences, it was still so easy for me to see through them to her kind gentle soul.

Meeting her friends later on revealed that I was really lucky to have had her open up to me the way she did on the first day we met. Being the first of six children, she was strict and hard core but all of that dissipated when she was with me.

I couldn't shake off what had happened the first day I met Purist; the day when I had heard it in my spirit: "*Do you know she could actually be your wife?*"

I had never heard God speak so clearly to me, and because it was a question, it left me confused for a while. What did God intend? Was she my wife, or not?

I hadn't even been searching for a wife at the time. Yes, I had been praying about marriage, but for the *future*; I just didn't realise the *future* had arrived! The prompt in my heart came as a shock and I had to watch the entire process of getting to know Purist over the next few months, wondering where God was leading us.

I was praying too, speaking with my pastors, my parents, my friends, all just to make sure I wasn't missing anything. And I wasn't. I got confirmation from all sides.

Being a person who is crazy about doing the will of God, I literally searched for the will of God in everything I did.

Later that year, I released my debut album, and I marvelled at how my life literally took off after meeting Purist.

I wasn't sure how it was going to pan out, but I was certain that all I had to do was follow God's leading. I put my heart into God's hands, and I decided to trust Him completely.

9

Purist

2007. Lagos, Nigeria.

The project had long been concluded, but Evans and I had forged a strong friendship, and we were getting *too close.*

Most of the time, we were in separate cities or locations, and we spoke mostly on the phone, but I was getting too emotionally entangled, and I was scared of what was happening.

We had such a meshing of our spirits, our likes, our thoughts, our dreams, it was amazing. The thought of what if something happened, and I got hurt, or he got hurt, always came up once in a while, and although I tried pulling away several times, I found it almost impossible.

Somehow, I would find a reason to call, he would find a reason to respond – the project was over, my single was ready, but our friendship was full and blossoming, and nowhere near ending. Evans never spoke about having feelings for me, or anything of the sort – our conversation was always about what was happening in our lives, our dreams and aspirations, our relationships with God, and yes a chunk of it was about music.

I wasn't sure what was going on. We were friends, or where we more than friends? What exactly where we doing? We spent time talking about so many things, our conversations were innocent, inspiring and uplifting, but they left me wanting more, desiring more, and I was not sure what to do.

I never forgot what God's spirit had spoken into my heart so tenderly that first meeting with Evans: *this is the one you have been praying for.*

My heart skipped a beat as I thought about it. *Was he the one?*

The more time I had spent with him, the more I wanted to spend more time with him. Could I dare hope that Evans and I would end up together? I didn't want to think about it, but it taunted my mind. If this was what God had said, then there had to be some form of a confirmation.

I remember praying and saying: Lord, *if this is really you, I want Evans and I to talk about what's happening between us.*

The next time Evans called, strangely, our conversation steered in a bizarre manner, and we got talking about the first day we met. I don't know how the words came out, but somehow, he told me what God had spoken in his heart and how he had told his friend about it.

God had said I could be his wife! I couldn't believe what I was hearing.

With a shaky, almost breathless voice, I told him about what I had heard in my spirit that same day, and how I had gone home to tell my siblings. I told him that was the reason I had almost choked on my drink.

He was suddenly quiet.

There was so much to ponder over.

Lord, what does this mean?

My heart was beating so loudly, I was certain he could hear it through the telephone.

Could this be real?

God had spoken to me, the same time He had spoken to him.

That conversation changed everything for us.

Evans

2007. Lagos, Nigeria.

I was standing by the balcony, holding my phone. The last strains of my conversation with Purist lingered in my heart.

I couldn't believe what had just happened.

What were the odds that she would have the same convictions that I had too, and at the same time as mine?

It was such a WOW moment. It all felt unbelievable, like a fairy-tale.

Do things like this happen?

Lord, who is this person? What have I done to deserve someone as awesome as she is?

She was all I prayed for, and even more. She was like a dream come true.

She was absolutely perfect, and each time I spoke with her, I just wanted to spend more time with her. She always spoke prophetically into my life, without even knowing it.

A few days later, we met in person to talk about the conversation we had on the phone. We knew that we could never go back to the way things had been.

Transitioning from being acquaintances to being in a relationship was not a difficult process because we already knew we were meant to be together, so it made it a lot easier.

The Holy Spirit had already done the work, we had both received a word from Him, on the same day. All we did from then on was pray that God would perfect what He had started in us. And that was how we shifted into a proper relationship.

For the first time, we held hands, and we prayed, and asked that if this relationship was not God's will, then things would not work – we would draw apart and go our separate ways, but if it was His will, He will stand with us, direct us, lead us, and give us the grace and strength to move on to the next level.

That day, standing there, with our hands united in prayer, it was as though the heavens and earth stood still as we said our prayers.

10

Purist

2011. Asaba, Nigeria.

Evans had proposed, and I had said yes! It was finally happening, and it only made sense that the families should meet officially, and get to know each other.

My father had different plans.

The day Evan's father was scheduled to come and visit, my father said he didn't want to hear me talk about marriage or any relationship until I had graduated from college.

I felt I was mature enough to consider getting married, I had recently decided to opt out of my course of study and pursue music, so in a sense, I had spent time growing and maturing. But my father didn't quite agree.

I was so angry with him, but he was my father and he put his foot down, vehemently.

Evans and I had no choice but to hang on until I had graduated. He had to wait for five years.

The minute I graduated from school in London, my father spoke to me on the phone, and after his congratulatory message, he added an interesting clause: "Bring the young man you said you want to marry, let him come and see me!"

Wow! I was elated. Evans at the time was also in London, studying Creative Media and Audio Production at SAE institute London.

Evans and I travelled to Nigeria to see my dad, there was so much ease, and tension – this was a meeting we had waited and prayed would happen for five years.

I secretly wondered how this meeting would go – they were the two most important men in my life, and I wanted things to work out well – everything depended on it.

God saw my heart, and heard my little prayer. On the day Evans and my dad met, they hit it off! Their meeting was so successful, they fixed the dates for our traditional engagement ceremony and our church wedding, on the same day!

It was incredulous – I only had four months to plan a wedding, but

I was so excited. This was what we had been praying for, and we couldn't wait to get married!

Evans went back to London because he had to go back to school, and I was left to run around to prepare for the wedding. I had planned to order my wedding dress from London, but there was still a lot of planning to be done, and it was my absolute joy!

I just couldn't wait to get started. Finally, I was going to be a bride!

Evans

2011. Asaba, Nigeria

Things had happened so quickly, I couldn't believe it.

As I boarded a plane, destination Nigeria to finally be joined in holy matrimony to the love of my life, I was just so grateful to God for His mercies.

Somehow, it had happened – we had come a long way from where we had been. I still couldn't believe we were getting married – so much had happened within that year.

That was the year that I had been admitted into SAE, one of the leading schools in Audio and Engineering and Music Production in the UK, and I had gone ahead to study.

Purist was also in London, so it had been quite the reunion. She had been studying Vocals and Music Performance at BIMM Tech Music School, London. Her dad had insisted that she had to graduate from college before introducing any *man* to him, so I had to wait for about five years before even meeting her dad!

I still remember only less than two years ago, I had been trusting God to gain admission into SAE institute London to study Creative Media and Audio Production, Purist had encouraged me to apply but I was considering the funding and other factors.

However, God spoke to me clearly somewhere around Ogba in Lagos, as I commuted from a friend's house.

What about SAE?

I knew it was God speaking, and I immediately went back home and straight to the cyber cafe.

I had signed up on the SAE mailing list a couple of months ago, and I received information from time to time. As I checked through my emails that day, I stumbled on an email I had overlooked from SAE. I scanned through the mail, it was a memo that indicated that they were now fully admitting international students.

I responded straight away!

At the time, all I had saved in the bank was about N200,000 which turned out to be the exact naira equivalence that I needed to register.

I sent the money and my documents to the school, and BOOM! A few weeks afterwards, I received an email with the good news: I had been admitted!

Now all that was left was for me to pay my full tuition fees, and somehow, we made it happen, and in the year of 2011, both of us were in London!

That same year I got into college was the year Purist was to graduate, and we desired to get married that year, 2011.

It didn't make sense because I hadn't met Purist's dad yet, and I still had all the formalities to get over with, but we kept speaking the word and prophesying that we were getting married that year.

And then miraculously, we got a break that year, just when she finished her degree, her dad requested to see me – he was finally ready!

We flew back to Nigeria in August, had our introduction, and fixed our wedding date for December, and everything just fell into place. We all just prayed that God's will be done.

And here I was, only four months later, flying back to be married.

I couldn't wait to see Purist, and I couldn't wait for us to finally begin our lives together!

Purist

2011. Asaba, Nigeria.

On the night before my wedding, I was unable to sleep.

I had waited for five years for this day to arrive.

The day had been a long one, and the traditional wedding had taken place on that day. Anyone would have expected that I would be tired, but my eyes shone awake. I could almost count the hours, minutes and seconds till I would finally get to say *I do.*

And finally, the sun rose, and the day finally began. As I wore my wedding dress and put the finishing touches to my looks, I felt my hands tingle with so much excitement.

It was finally happening!

My mind cast back to the God had spoken a word into my heart about Evans: *this is the one you have been praying for!*

I couldn't thank God enough for giving me a man like Evans. In the past five years that I had known him, I had not met a better man.

He had the fear of God, and there were certain things that stood out for me – his caring nature, he was very nice, a proper gentleman, and he was kind-hearted. The one that got me was that he was a lover of God – he was completely sold out, and I deeply admired that he was a true Christian man. And that was the man I was marrying.

I stood before the mirror, and took in my looks.

The white dress fitted around my waist, and its satin form fell around my body, and curved into a beautiful ball gown finish. The lace veil was draped over my face to finish my bridal look. This was it! I was ready!

The phone next to me buzzed. It was Evans. I smiled as I read his text, and I quickly replied with another text of mine. We had been texting back and forth in the last few hours.

For the bulk of our relationship, we had been far apart, and we had spent most of the relationship on the phone, or texting. The thought of finally being able to be together was something we had prayed for, and yearned for so long a time.

I got ready very early, much earlier than everyone else.

They wondered because usually, the bride was the last to get ready. This bride couldn't wait to get married!

I hoisted up my dress and went to find my father.

A few minutes later, seated next to him, he drove me to church.

There were no fancy things, not so much drama, or crazy frenzy. We didn't have a long bridal train, just a chief bridesmaid and a best man. We were so crazy about each other, even if there was no one at the venue, but ourselves and the pastor, we would have been eager and happy to get married.

As I walked into the church, I still couldn't believe it was really happening. My parents beamed with pride, I could almost sense the emotions in their hearts as they watched their *baby girl*, walking down the aisle, prepared to be joined in holy matrimony, and become a woman of her own.

Evans stood at the far end, looking dapper in his suit, with touches of orange and green, to compliment the orange and green colour theme we had chosen for the wedding.

The ceremony was simple, traditional and it proceeded like a breeze. The Lead Pastor from RCCG Living Faith Connections, the pastor of the church where we worshipped and served in London had flown in from the UK to perform the joining ceremony, and he led us to say our vows to each other.

We stood, holding hands, and before our friends, and family, we pledged our hearts and lives to each other.

I had goose bumps all over, and butterflies in my tummy as we said our vows.

After our vows, everything moved on quickly; the Pastor delivered a brief sermon, we signed the marriage registry, the entire congregation prayed for us, and of course, lots of dancing and celebration followed.

Minutes later, as we marched out of the church, ring in my finger, wife of Evans Ogboi, I still couldn't get over what had just happened – I couldn't believe I was finally married to the man of my dreams.

It felt like I was floating, I felt like I was dreaming – was this really happening?

As we took pictures at the poolside of the hotel where we had our reception, everything still felt strange, like a haze.

My sisters were around me, their faces were filled with smiles, and joy. It was such a happy, beautiful day.

The reception was a beautiful little hall that had been arranged with tables and chairs clothed in white. The guests were already seated in the hall when Evans and I officially arrived at the reception, and there was another round of jubilant dancing and merry making.

In the midst of it all – the excitement, and delight, I paused to look at Evans. He looked so happy, so peaceful, he turned to look at me.

Thank you Jesus for this precious gift, I muttered inwardly. He had worked all things together for our good.

This indeed, was the day the Lord had made!

This was one of my happiest days!

Evans

2011. Asaba, Nigeria.

Everyone dreams of having the perfect wedding, having fireworks up in the sky, shutting down ten streets and even walking on water if possible. That had been my dream for my wedding.

It was a few days after our wedding, and looking back at the event, I was happy with the work that Purist had put into preparing for the wedding.

Of course, we had big dreams for our wedding but we had to wake up to the realities of our finances and put priorities in place, choosing to focus on the marriage beyond the wedding day.

A lot of the preparation for our wedding was handled by Purist, I was in the UK at the time, and she was back home in Nigeria.

We made plans over the phone and over *Skype*, on how the wedding day would go, and this went on up until a day before the wedding when I flew into the country, straight to *Asaba,* the town where Purist and her parents lived, and where the wedding was going to take place.

Purist had somehow managed to pull off the organisation of our wedding in four months, and we had a wonderful day. A few friends had flown into the country to celebrate with us including my pastor from London, Pastor Chris Adeoye, Lead Pastor RCCG

Living Faith Connections.

I remember being at my wedding reception, amidst the celebration, reminding myself that I was actually getting married. I was overjoyed, I was lost. It was a dream come true. Everyone was congratulating me, it was such a beautiful day; I almost couldn't remember the faces at my wedding because of how ecstatic I felt.

I had always lived with the fear of who I was going to get married to, and how her family would be, but all that was taken care of by God.

I married a preacher's kid, my father-in-law is such a great man, my mother-in-law is amazing, and her siblings are like angels.

I was simply just overwhelmed, and I was caught up with the emotions of the day.

I was a young man who didn't have much; all I had was a dream which the grace of God brought to life.

When I met Purist, I didn't have anything. I had actually told her the first time she showed up at my studio that everything she saw there – a computer and a few other things – were all I had to my name, but it was enough to keep us happy.

I remember a time, a few years before we were married, when we were both on a commercial motorcycle, heading to a church in Obalende, Lagos to minister, and we were laughing so hard I thought to myself: *if we are this happy when we're broke, how much more when we become wealthy?*

I thought of how we had evolved from the first time we met, into our relationship, and now marriage.

During our relationship, we'd laugh at each other, and do things to make each other laugh; we were ourselves, we were just friends and I remember Purist telling me that she had prayed to have that with her husband, the kind of friendship David had with Jonathan; and God answered that prayer.

Purist was the first of six children, and I was really proud of how she was raised. One of the values Purist was taught was to never look for a man that was *already-made* but to choose a man that she could build life with, and grow with.

Purist had come from a pretty comfortable family and so choosing to be with *some guy* who had nothing but a dream to be a music producer was amazing.

I had watched her disposition over the years, and seeing how content she was, how happy she was every time, was such an encouragement to me. That's one of the qualities I loved the most. God had indeed sent her into my life – the bone of my bone and flesh of my flesh!

There were a couple of hurdles ahead of us. I was leaving for the UK soon, and she was going to remain here in Nigeria until we could figure out how she could join me.

I was confident that God who had started with us would lead us through to the very end. There was so much more to come, we had just started the page of our lives together, and there was so much waiting for us ahead, together.

We would conquer all – Purist and I; together, our love would win, come what may.

11

Evans & Purist

Being married is one of the best things that happened to us, especially being married to each other – we are each other's best friend! It is our desire that everyone finds a greater measure of the happiness and joy we have found in marriage. The love, the contentment, sincerity, transparency, unity and the focus we share are the things that inspire us about our marriage.

The devil fights the institution of marriage, and there are a lot of attacks targeted at marriage, because he knows that the family is the fabric of the society.

Marriages are attacked even before they begin. Many young people are scared of getting married. Everywhere they turn, they see marriage models that portray suffering, endurance and gloom, and their fear drives them to make the wrong decisions in choosing a spouse.

In every marriage, God should remain the anchor, and just like the song: '*my hope is built on nothing less*', marriage partners should rest upon God, and make God their anchor in marriage.

To build and sustain your marriage, and get it to stand and thrive, your prayer life has to be strong; your communication with God needs to remain constant.

Finding *The One*

For the single person who is reading this book, and is wondering where *the one* is, remember that God already knew you before sending you into this world; He already orchestrated the details of your life.

For this reason, it is wise to go back to God, your manufacturer and study your manual, which is the word of God. You need to go back to God and ask Him who you are to marry. We can't overemphasize how important this is. If this is gotten right, every other thing will fall into place.

We encourage you to seek the face of God, simply ask Him; this has worked for us – that's our testimony.

You might have an uncanny feeling that God won't give you

someone you like and desire, and that's simply not true, God will give you what you desire and even more, He'd give you what you didn't even know you liked.

So, seek God, trust Him, allow Him help you make that decision, let this process of finding *the one*, be in His will, when you find *that one*, you will walk into rest for the entirety of your marriage.

Marriage is not to be rushed into. It's something to take your time, and pray carefully about. Ask God for guidance, and even after you've met *the one,* seek confirmation from spiritual leaders, and God will perfect everything concerning you.

Building and Growing Your Marriage

God has the blueprint of our lives and for every marriage; and so we need to seek him daily, as individuals but also as a family. Only He can renew a marriage covenant.

The word of God as well has played a strong role in sustaining our own marriage. Understanding what God is saying to us specifically, seeking daily direction and being led has brought us peace and joy.

Communicating effectively has also helped to build our marriage to the point where it is today.

Finding Peace In Marriage.

Are you in a troubled marriage?

Are things spiralling out of control?

Do you desire peace in your marriage?

We believe in the efficacy of the word of God – there's really nothing impossible for Him and it's only wise that you trust Him in your marriage.

The bible records all the amazing miracles He did and we can always use that as a reference in reaching out to Him in prayer for our marriages.

Asides prayer, try to make amends in your relationship with your spouse. You can't always be right, and you can't possibly know everything; you'd have to learn about yourself, learn about your spouse, and learn how to be a better spouse.

Do all you can to make your home into what you want it to be.

Whatever you're seeing in your marriage that is not desirable, take it to God in prayers, the bible says to *Cast all our cares on Him for He cares for us*, and *be anxious for nothing but in all things, in prayer and thanksgiving let your prayers be known unto God*.

Pray, knowing God will answer; and pray, actually looking out for the answer.

If you're believing God for the salvation or deliverance of your spouse, pray, and trust the Lord. Saul was a staunch persecutor of Christians but ended up being one of the most zealous preachers of the gospel. There's nothing God cannot do, confess the word, trust God.

Believe God for a beautiful marriage, and you will walk into it.

Section Three:

Journey To Parenthood
2012 - 2017

12

Evans

2012. London, UK

It was three months after our wedding, and I was back in Nigeria after being away from my wife. I was as glad as a newly married man who was just seeing his wife again could be.

I had just finished studying and we were trying to get Purist to the UK to join me, so having a child wasn't the first thing on our minds then, settling down was.

I didn't think parenthood would happen immediately; I wanted us to wait till we were financially ready and so, I didn't have any immediate plans. I looked forward to being a father, and I desired that my children would be better than I was, and would have more than I ever had growing up.

We planned to have a certain number of children, children who we could take care of effectively and raise in the way of the Lord, and children we could be there for in every way possible.

As of the time, I was working on a project, and Purist was also working alongside me. As a result, we had to go to the studio frequently, and I noticed Purist was always tired and sleepy, but didn't think much of it at the time.

We got Purist's papers sorted out and headed back to the UK, and a few days afterwards, we went to have dinner at a Chinese restaurant.

While we were eating, she complained that she was feeling a sharp pain in her tummy, and we concluded it was the strong spices in the food, and took note never to visit that restaurant.

Days later, we discovered the good news! We were pregnant!

It wasn't planned but still I was ecstatic, this was a welcome surprise!

Purist

2012. London, UK

I was excited!

Who would have thought all the time I was feeling dizzy that I was actually pregnant? Two months pregnant to be precise. I had become pregnant before leaving Nigeria.

It was an exciting discovery, it was kind of strange, and I remember going to my Pastor's wife and telling her I felt I had changed. A wide smile spread across her face as she congratulated me – "God has done it for you! Do you know how many people are waiting for a miracle like this?"

Shortly afterwards, I began to have intense pains in my stomach. I was not sure if this was meant to happen during pregnancy.

I went to the hospital, and the doctors said the pain was coming from a large cyst that had attached itself to my left ovary. The doctors were confident that the pregnancy could be managed, but they would have to bring the baby out by 28 weeks.

Throughout the pregnancy, I experienced heavy bleeding, and as the pregnancy progressed, it got really bad and I started also clotting too. I had to use pads continually, and every visit to the toilet was a scary experience for me.

The doctors said it was a high risk pregnancy, and for the next couple of weeks, I was in and out of the hospital, always on admission, and constantly receiving drips and fluids.

On the Sunday that changed everything, I woke up in pains. I was about fifteen weeks pregnant. Evans had gone off to church and had left me behind because I had not been feeling very strong. I couldn't go to church that day, and we decided that I stay home and rest.

The pains intensified to a point that it became unbearable. I began to scream and shout, and it was almost as if I was going crazy. There was no one at home, and no one to come to my aid. I picked up the phone and with quivering fingers, dialled Evan's number. It was ringing. He was not picking up.

He was at the peak of the Sunday Service, which was usually jostling with praise, worship and all sorts. It might be hours before he picked up his phone.

I called other people to try to get to him.

I also called an ambulance.

Why are they taking forever to get here? My thoughts drifted into a haze from random thoughts. The pain was intense, I felt like I was going to go crazy from pain.

Lord, where are you? Lord, help me…

Evans

2012. London, UK

I was in church, when suddenly, I got a call telling me my wife was in pains and I needed to rush home.

Frantic, I dashed home as soon as I possibly could, and I met Purist in excruciating pain. Unexplainable thoughts ran through my head.

What's happening here?

I called the ambulance but I was too impatient to answer their many questions, it was hard to think straight amidst the cries and screams from my wife, somehow, we managed to get a cab and rushed her to the hospital.

After hours of waiting, we were told that the ovarian cyst had twisted and had a high risk of rupturing. She had to be operated upon immediately, or we risked losing her.

It felt like a scary movie of some sort.

I was there, alone, seated along the hospital corridor, my mind thinking of a zillion things while trying to get in touch with her parents and update them on all that was happening.

Moments later, I watched her, in so much pain, being wheeled to the theatre, I was too mortified to cry, I didn't know how to. How had everything taken a drastic turn so quickly?

One minute I was at church lifting holy hands, the next I was watching my wife, in a hospital gown, being wheeled into surgery. It was too much for my mind to comprehend. I tried not to think.

Hours later, the doctor explained the situation to us.

They had taken out my wife's left ovary and fallopian tube. I sat there, my head spinning.

Purist

2012. London, UK

The next thing I remember was a voice speaking in a distance. It was the doctor.

"You will hear your name, and you will come back... Purist.... Purist...'

My eyelids fluttered, I looked up, and I could feel motion as I was being wheeled from the theatre. When I finally awoke, Evans was seated by my side. He was still dressed in his Sunday best – now creased and rumpled, worry impressed on his face, his hands clasped together in prayer.

The doctor broke the news to me and Evans. They had to cut out the cyst, but because it was too big, they had to cut it out along with the ovary and fallopian tube it had attached itself to.

But the baby had managed to survive, and we hung unto this shred of hope, believing God that things would work out for good.

Evans

2012. London, UK

We went home and tried to work through all that had happened, we prayed and kept hope alive, our child was still alive and when there was life, there was hope! Even though the doctor had told us the worst was still ahead we clung to our faith, and we were certain all will be well.

After a few days, bleeding started, followed by frequent visits to the hospital which ended in the eventual loss of the pregnancy.

The loss was excruciating, horrific, to say the least.

We got to decide how our first pregnancy was going to end.

We sat there, mortified, and listened to the options the doctor gave. My wife could either be injected and go through labour and delivery, or be operated upon. Either way, our baby was not going to live.

Nothing in this world could have compared to the pain we felt at that point.

Imagine having to decide how your unborn baby was going to die.

My wife was in pain. She was at the hospital going through the horror of delivering our lifeless child that hadn't even gotten the chance to develop completely.

Purist

2012. London, UK

The next few days were slow, painful and the road to recovery was ahead. We still believed our baby would be fine. A few weeks afterwards, the bleeding started, and I had to be rushed back to the hospital.

We had fought so hard, so long, but at the end of it all, the doctors broke the news to us - our baby was not going to survive this.

I was in a haze. Why was this happening?

We had been sold out to Christ. We were die-hard Christians.

Why? We pay out tithes. Lord, please give me a reason why this is happening.

In Africa, when things happened, we were always found a reason why. There was always a village curse somewhere, and a reason for things to happen. We searched for our reason why. We were born again Christians, we had lived our lives for God, we had stayed true and committed to our walk with God – why then, was this happening? Why was it happening to us?

We called our parents, and we asked them what they thought we should do.

They couldn't make a decision for us, and we had to decide for ourselves.

It was the hardest decision to make.

I couldn't go through another surgery, because I had just come out of one a few weeks ago. So I had to take the option of delivering the baby. I was given a drug that brought an onset of labour. I went through the pain and agony of labour, and afterwards, brought forth a breathless baby.

This was not what I had envisaged when I thought of motherhood. This was not supposed to happen.

Why is this happening to me?

I couldn't understand it, I couldn't fathom it.

"Do you want to hold the baby?" the nurses had asked me, sympathy in their eyes.

It seemed like a good idea. It would give me a chance to say goodbye, they had said, and in a brief second, I also agreed with them. I nodded in response.

Evans couldn't stand it. He rose to his feet, and excused himself.

The nurses brought the lifeless baby to me. I held what had been a part of me, what had grown in me, I held our child close, I brought it to my heart, and the pain filtered through my body as I wept silently.

This was the beginning of the madness.

13

Evans

2012. London, UK

Eventually, we were discharged and left for home with our spirits down but as we journeyed home that day, I heard in my spirit that I wasn't even supposed to return home with my wife.

The devil had much more bigger plans of stealing my joy, and truncating my destiny in a much more grand style. The whole situation was meant to take Purist out, and leave me a widower, just barely six months after marriage. I was actually blessed to still have my wife, alive, well, and breathing, beside me.

Glory to God!

'Where there's life, there's hope!' My spirit found solace in those words, I found strength in the fact that the enemy meant to steal my joy by taking my wife, but here she was.

I gave thanks, and for the first time in the midst of the trauma we had experienced, I breathed deeply, and said *'Thank You Jesus.'*

I repeated it over and over again, as I allowed the thought of what might have been, and how much worse it could have gone, drive me into a period of thanksgiving.

I was assured that somehow God had a plan, He was working all things for our good, and He would help us get through this.

Purist

2012. London, UK

When we got back home, the reality of what had happened hit me, and it hit me so hard. As I opened the door, the memories I had of the excitement and anticipation of our baby came flooding back to me, and the thought settled deep within. There was no baby. The baby was gone.

We lived in a three story building, and I wanted to hurl myself over the balcony. I wanted to die. I just began to wail, I couldn't be comforted. *My baby was gone!*

Evans was thrown into a panic, his face was etched with worry, confusion, he was calling people on the phone to talk to me, and he was trying to hold unto me. He was beside himself, as he begged me to take a hold of myself.

I was going crazy, losing my mind, losing myself, and then I looked at him, and just froze momentarily. He looked exhausted, tired and drained of all his energy. I had never seen him like this.

Love and compassion for him just oozed from my heart, and I stopped fighting and struggling, and collapsed in a heap.

He gathered me in his arms, and we cried together.

I apologized.

We just sat in each other's arms, and cried.

Somehow, we managed to get through that night, but somewhere during the nights that followed, I slowly began to slide into depression.

At certain times, I would suddenly remember that I was no longer pregnant, I would touch my tummy where the baby had been, and I would sink into a sour mood. It could happen anywhere – sometimes it happened in the middle of a conversation, or in the middle of watching a movie, or just doing the regular things that had once brought me so much joy.

I was gradually losing myself, and losing touch with who I was.

Evans remained a strong support system. Through all I experienced, he never *flipped.* Sometimes, I cried, I ranted; I withdrew to myself, and didn't speak a word for hours – sometimes, I couldn't even recognise who I had become. Every time I looked at Evans, he brought me back to myself – he always had this look of tenderness, his eyes would bore through mine, just oozing with so much compassion and concern for me.

I just wanted to be strong, for him, just so he wouldn't have to suffer so much. I was trying so hard to be strong but every day, I felt like I was slipping away even further.

We decided that we would get through this, together. We would make this work, we would hold our hands and with the help of God, we would find a way out of this blizzard, together.

14

Evans

2013. London, UK

And then we got pregnant again!

It was a miracle considering that an ovary and a fallopian tube had been removed. This was God's doing!

We were overjoyed, elated. It had happened.

Sadly, that baby didn't come to stay and so we lost it, quite early too. Before we had time to fully experience the miracle, it was gone, snatched from us, again.

Purist

2013. London, UK

Then the second pregnancy came. We were so excited. This was truly a miracle!

And then the bleeding started.

And then it was gone.

15

Evans

2014. London, UK

And then the third.

It was hard to make sense of it.

Three pregnancies.

Three babies.

Three miracles.

All gone.

Even worse, it happened on days when we had major events, big concerts, days we had been scheduled to minister, bring down the presence of God, those were the days our joy was stolen.

Purist

2014. London, UK

When we got the news that we were pregnant for the third time, we were scared. We were not taking any chances this time, and I was taking things very easy.

Evans was about to release his album, and everything was going well.

On the night of his album release, the bleeding started.

The following morning, I got to the hospital, and the doctors told us – we had lost our baby, again.

16

Evans

2015. London, UK

And then the fourth.

This time we were determined to hold it – hold our baby so tight no force in hell could take it away from us.

We prayed every day, and we got a word from the Lord through a friend and she told my wife: '*This one will stay.*' This became our watch word, and we held unto it.

This one will stay!

Maybe we hadn't been praying hard enough for the other three, maybe all we needed this time was *a word from God*, maybe we didn't decree the word as often as we should have. This time though, we were not taking any chances, we prayed and prayed and prayed.

I had a program at Sunderland where I was to minister in music, and I was supposed to be gone for two days leaving my wife alone at home.

A few minutes before I left the house, she complained of seeing a little red spot and I wasn't having it – I rebuked the devil immediately and decreed the word, told her not to let the fear grow and bear fruits in her heart. She insisted on going to the hospital for check-up, just to be sure everything was fine. I agreed with that, and asked her to keep me updated.

I kissed her goodbye, and left for Sunderland.

Purist

2015. London, UK

After Evans left, I went to the hospital for a check-up, but I had a heart filled with faith. I was determined not to let anything get me down. This baby was here to stay!

The doctors decided to run a scan, just to make sure everything was fine. In the middle of the scan, the technician's face suddenly went pale. I knew something was up. "What's going on?" I asked.

He didn't respond. He left the scanning machine, and someone else came in to check the scan report, and conduct another scan. By the time the second personnel left and a senior personnel came in, I knew something had happened.

"What's happening?"

No one said anything to me. But I knew something was wrong.

I started crying.

God this can't be happening.

"Are you alone?" he finally asked. "Do you have family members? Where is your husband?"

My fear began to grow. "My husband travelled, he just travelled today."

He paused, and sighed deeply before continuing slowly. "From the result of the scan, the baby has stopped growing… and we can't find a heartbeat…"

This sounded all too familiar. This couldn't be happening. Not again!

The doctor gave me the option to take a drug to induce labour, or give birth naturally. They said labour could happen naturally.

"I can't make this decision on my own," I said shakily, "my

husband will be back the following day, we'll decide what to do then."

I believed that the Lord would turn this around. It didn't matter what they were telling me, this was our miracle baby. *This one would stay!*

Evans

Sunderland, UK

The first night of the program was a dinner and I was scheduled to minister. It was a bow-tie event. The guests had arrived – everyone was dressed looking beautiful and radiant, the atmosphere was amazing and I was super charged.

I took the microphone and by God's grace, I ministered powerfully, with so much joy in my heart. My joy was overflowing as I ministered that night, I felt heaven come down and it wasn't just me. Everyone testified of how amazing my ministration went, and I was smiling from ear to ear.

Amidst the praise celebration, my phone rang – it was Purist. I dashed out to pick the call, excited to tell my wife of how amazing the night had been. Straining to hear my wife's voice because of the noise coming from the church, I moved a little farther away, down on the streets of Sunderland.

That was when I heard it, the tearful voice of my wife that in recent times, I had come to know so well.

My heart sank as she said those words, *"They can't find the heartbeat…they can't find our baby's heartbeat…"*

The cold wind washed over me as I held the phone to my ear, it was suddenly so cold, too cold. Standing there, on the brightly lit street of Sunderland in my black suit, black bowtie and black leather shoes, the entire world seemed to darken.

I wasn't sure what to think, what to do. I kept myself from sitting on the floor like a hopeless man. I was freezing, and I couldn't believe what I was hearing.

This was happening for the fourth time.

I was miles away and so I wasn't there to comfort my wife, I myself needed to be comforted.

I was here to minister this weekend, my guests were inside, what was I supposed to do? Go inside and tell them I couldn't stay the entire weekend? My head swarmed with confusion.

I called back my wife and she was crying, crying so badly. I kept myself from breaking down in tears too because she needed me to be strong for her.

As I comforted her over the phone, I felt something die in me. I was broken and my soul was tired.

As we ended the phone call and I walked into the church, I felt different from the man who had walked out just a few minutes ago. I felt empty as though something had left me.

I muttered a silent prayer under my breath and asked God to simply see me through the rest of the evening. I tried to smile and put up a good front for those I shared a table with, but deep down, my heart was wrenching in pain.

Once the event ended, I walked into my hotel room with the weight of the world on my shoulders.

This is the fourth time, I kept thinking. *How can this be the fourth time? How? Why?*

I had so many questions with no answers, so I settled in and called Purist to inform her that I would be on my way home the next morning. With her tired voice she told me not to bother but instead I should finish my ministration and just return home after it had ended, because there really was no point.

I shouldn't have listened though.

17

Purist

2015. London, UK.

That evening after I returned from the hospital, I started spotting again.

I went on the internet and read everything I possibly could, hoping it would stop. Then the pain started. It was so intense, I knew I had to go to the hospital.

I called the ambulance, and before it arrived, I tried to reach Rev Funke Felix-Adejumo, a dear spiritual mother to myself and Evans. I had to call her son, Gbenga, and ask him to reach his mother for me. "I think I'm having a miscarriage," I told him in a shaky voice. "I need you to get Mama to pray for me."

And then it happened, right there in the living room.

There was no one around, the pain was severe, and I laboured, through tears and screams, and birthed the lifeless baby myself.

I packed the tiny baby with trembling hands, I held it in my palm. I was so confused.

Where do I put the baby? In the kitchen? On the table? In the fridge?

I finally decided to put it in the garden, and so I buried it in the backyard.

Afterwards, I had to pass out the placenta.

Several minutes later, when the ambulance arrived, the attendants analysed the situation in silent shock.

I was sprawled on the couch, I had lost a considerable amount of blood, was weak and extremely tired.

They wanted to take the foetus away and asked me where it was. I replied that I had buried it in the garden.

They looked at me, with bewilderment and confusion. They put me on oxygen, strapped me to a stretcher and rushed me to the hospital.

Evans

2015. London, UK.

The next day, I went for my concert and ministered just as powerful as the night before but this time I didn't minister out of joy to the Lord, it was out of anger at the devil, so much burning anger at the vices of the devil.

The concert was over and I was headed for London. Apparently Purist had been home still believing God for a miracle for our child inside of her, our child with no heartbeat.

She had been praying so hard, calling all the pastors she could call worldwide, frantically holding unto hope. She found a way to reach Rev Funke Felix-Adejumo and amidst tears, begged her to pray for her, which Mama did.

She was crying all through this, crying, but still believing God for a miracle.

After all was said and done, she was left to face reality. All alone in the house, she delivered our dead baby, dug a hole behind our home in the garden, and laid it to rest there, all by herself.

I got back home and went straight to the hospital, there I heard all about what had happened and I could barely believe my wife had gone through all that, alone. I wasn't sure how she could be alright after everything she had gone through. I kept asking her if she was

OK and she kept affirming.

The toughest part was calling our parents to let them know what was happening.

18

Purist

2015. London, UK.

After the fourth miscarriage, I didn't want to speak to any family member, my siblings or my mum, or dad. I was tired of hearing the same consolation.

"It's well..."

I was tired of hearing *God understands...*

I was tired of hearing *God will do it again... which God?*

I was in a place that I wouldn't wish for anyone.

A few weeks later, I had recovered, my body had healed but my mind was in a mess. I couldn't get the image of the two babies we had lost from my head. I had seen them, held them, and for the briefest of moments, I had loved them; their faces haunted my dreams, taunted me, and almost drove me to the point of insanity.

Meanwhile, we went to the hospital, and several investigations were conducted, trying to find out what was wrong, and what was responsible for all the miscarriages. The tests were extensive, but they couldn't find anything. I wished something was wrong, so we could at least have a particular ailment to treat.

After all the blood work, all the manners of prodding, after they had conducted every test, the doctors couldn't find anything medically wrong.

Evans

2015. London, UK.

I had gone to minister at a concert on this particular day, just after we had had one of the miscarriages and we were dealing with the loss.

Crying didn't come naturally to me. I wasn't the type of guy to cry when I was in pain but on this particular day, being In the presence of God, I was moved to lay it out there.

I cried my eyes and heart out, I showed my soul to God. Every song began to take on a new meaning, as I lifted up my hands and worshipped.

My turn came to minister and I did, so powerfully. This was how I grieved.

For Purist, it was a lot harder, she cried almost every day, she was always crying. Dealing with all the losses was so draining, as individuals and as a couple. I was constantly praying for my wife, praying for strength, praying that God will keep her mind sound.

Praying became hard, devotions became tough. It was tough because the devotions sometimes always told us to do things we had already done countless times.

Trust God.

Pray.

Believe.

We had done all those things in the past, but still things had turned out the way they did.

On a particular day, we knelt down to pray but Purist kept crying, she tried but she couldn't help herself, she couldn't help the pain. I held her and begged her to try and she looked up to me with tired red eyes and said in a cracked voice '*Baby, help me, pray for me*'

I tried not to look at her, I tried to focus on praying but when I did, I saw her soul, I saw her soul dying, reaching out to be rescued like a drowning person would. I saw her trying frantically to hold on to hope, trying so hard to stay sane and believe.

It was at that point I knew we needed God to help us.

And I prayed.

I kept praying for God to strengthen us and keep us from losing our minds to this pain that seemed to be eating deep into our souls.

I prayed that God would keep our hearts and sustain our marriage.

On some days, when the house went silent and I hadn't seen Purist in more than a couple of minutes, I'd go searching for her, and for certain, I would find her somewhere, wiping her eyes, trying to feign a smile, to make me worry less. She was always crying, and that affected me.

Communicating and relating with some people became hard and we started to withdraw from them because they didn't seem to understand or know how to be sensitive to all we were going through.

We somehow found strength and joy in our friendship with each other. On some days, we found something random to laugh about, but the pain was a constant companion and after every joyful moment, the pain was there waiting to start every new day with us.

19

Evans

2016. London, UK.

The struggles to parenthood were enormous and one of the biggest issues I faced was being a Christian, being full of faith, being a minister of the gospel and still not being able to bear a child.

I was a worker in the house of God, a person who pointed others to Jesus, how could I explain it? How could I explain being so spirit filled but still having to deal with this situation?

The first challenge we had was uncertainty. If we had known what the problem was, what had gone wrong, we'd be a step closer to fixing it, but we didn't. We didn't know what the problem was, if it was this or that, and so it was hard to even channel our prayers. We didn't know what particular problem we should have been praying about.

There was so much confusion.

And then we began to grow weary, even in prayer. Particular prayer points started to make us cringe, and whenever prayers for those seeking the fruit of the womb were raised anywhere, the countenance of my wife would change.

Purist became sensitive and the subject of conceiving became such a touchy subject. Well-meaning friends would reach out to us and send us prayers and prophesies about having children but it just drove Purist farther and farther away.

She didn't want to talk about it, hear about it, she just wanted God to do what He wanted to do.

The bible says *hope deferred makes the heart sick*, but thank God for God, when we got into our ministry, when we got into worship, it made things a bit better.

Another part of the struggle was fear, a lot of which was due to the miscarriages we had to deal with in the past. It got to a point that every time we found out we were pregnant, instead of joy and excitement, we became afraid, thinking: '*What's going to happen this time?*' The fear was always there.

When you go through some certain trials and tests, you begin to doubt yourself, I got to that point.

I started to doubt myself, doubt my Christianity, doubt all that I had believed, all I had confessed in the past, the circumstance came and just ruffled my feathers.

I started to ask myself if I was even standing well: *is there a curse? Is it generational? Have I sinned? Is there something I need to repent of?*

Making declarations only gave the devil an opportunity to mock me, you know, whenever I'd make a declaration, the devil will whisper, '*are you sure? Isn't this how you made a declaration last month? Did it actually happen?*' Even in the place of prayer, my faith was running really low.

I never quite got to the point where I thought we'd never actually have a child but I battled with the thought once in a while, '*when is this thing going to end? When will our miracle happen?*'

I even remember saying to myself that if this took giving – giving money, giving anything, I'd give it. I knew this was something money couldn't buy but I had gotten to my wits end and really, there is nothing I wouldn't have given, nothing I wouldn't have done. At some point, I remember telling God: "Lord, *I'll do anything, just tell me what to do God, just tell me…*'

It reminds me of the man in the bible who when asked by Jesus if he believed, he said he did believe, but he needed Jesus to help his unbelief. I did believe, but I still needed God to help my unbelief.

My story was a lot like the man at the pool of Bethesda who had been there for thirty-eight years. I prayed all manner of prayers, fasted and the case wasn't that of not seeing the manifestation, it came and it left through the miscarriages we had.

The more miscarriages we had, the more it depleted our faith, it reduced us.

We then started to ask God for faith, strength to even believe.

20

Purist

2016. London, UK.

I was at a stage in my life where I had to do something to get my sanity back because I was losing it.

I was angry, I was hurting, and I had stopped believing in God. I knew that I was treading on dangerous ground – I was almost getting to a point where I was blaspheming.

I was an angry woman. Anyone that dared come near me at the time would feel the full wrath of my anger. I was angry and bitter. I cut off from my family, and I wasn't speaking to anyone.

It was that bad because I felt less of a woman.

Some of the people around me were not helping much at this time. Many times words were spoken insensitively during periods that I had just come out of a miscarriage, and these words broke me down, time and time again.

I turned to certain places and people, expecting to find some form of comfort, but instead, I found insensitivity, hurt and even more pain.

I had to learn how to apply make-up with just the right strokes, just so I could conceal my sorrow beautifully. I had mastered the art of makeup so no one would have to ask me: *are you okay? You're looking sad.* I invested in makeup to cover the bitterness. Even at that, I couldn't cover it up so perfectly.

Inwardly, my heart was crying out loud.

Lord, when will this end?

When will you bless me with a child?

When will this madness come to an end?

Evans

2016. London, UK.

We also faced struggles with several people who possibly had good intentions and meant well for us, but subconsciously had made plans for us, and had done their calculations on when certain events should take place. Based on these calculations, they were checking their personal calendars, and asking questions we didn't want to answer; questions that had become too painful to answer.

Are you guys planning to have children?

A huge chunk of our struggle was internal – having to meet people year after year without a change, we had tarried on this mountain for too long, carrying the shame of *stagnancy*, the appearance of *barrenness* when you believed firmly that you were not barren, and having to deal with situations that were constantly trying to pull down our faith.

This grew into super sensitivity, and we became irritated by every little thing, including the prayers of well meaning, loving people who greatly cared about our situation.

We had to constantly ask God to restore our hearts, restore the joy of our salvation, and see us through this dark season which seemed to have no end.

Purist

2016. London, UK.

Evans was continually praying for me. Evans had said several times, "Baby, you can't get your blessing where you are now, because you are hurting, bitter. You need to get healed."

I knew he was right. To receive my miracle, I needed to get rid of the pain, the anger, the hurt.

One morning during our devotion, I remember, the Holy Spirit spoke to my heart. This hadn't happened in a while and I knew it was time to let go of everything, my hurt, my grief, everything – even if letting go was going to be gradual process. I had to start from somewhere.

I went on my knees for the first time in a long time, and I could see my husband watching me, in surprise.

I said, "Babe, I want my heart to be healed, I want the hurt to leave, I want the images to leave, I just want to be healed, let God take these images from me, let God forgive me, I've not been praying…"

I had backslidden, and I had gone so far away from God. I said the prayer of forgiveness, and Evans led me back to Christ during one of our morning devotions.

The journey to my healing started from that day forward.

21

Purist

2016. London, UK.

God began to heal me, and take me through a journey.

I wanted my life back, and I began to ask the question - *What do I do? What gives me joy and pleasure?* I had to fall back to my first love – music.

For a while, I had stopped looking at people in the eye. I was always finding an excuse to put my head down. And even when I was in a crowded place, at an event, I would try not to get up in the middle of the event, even when I needed to use the rest room. I always felt like the world was watching me, and judging me. I had suddenly gone back to being the shy, fourteen year old with insecurities and low self-esteem that I had been back in high school.

I imagined everyone was mocking me, and I was ashamed because I couldn't bear children, I felt less of a woman.

All of that gradually stopped. I could now look up and confidently walk across a hallway without fear of being judged or condemned. Slowly and gradually, I began to get myself back.

One interesting thing began to happen.

In my sleep, the Lord began to minister to me through songs, lyrics and music. I would sleep and receive songs, and that was how *The Encounter* became a reality.

IDIRI-MU-MA.

I slept and woke up with the song, *Idiri-Mu-Ma.* It was in Igbo, one of the local dialects in Nigeria. Although I was Igbo, I was not a fluent speaker, and I didn't understand what the phrase meant, so I called my mom and asked her to help translate it. It turned out that it was a thanksgiving song.

I was a bit confused. Why would God give me a thanksgiving song? How do you sing a song of thanksgiving when you had *nothing* to be grateful for? It was then I learned that I needed to praise Him in the good and the bad, praise Him even when I had been through so much. At a point when I thought I had *nothing* to be grateful for, He showed me that I had *everything* to be grateful for – I had life, I had breath, and I had a promise of a better tomorrow.

The Vow was another song also given to me by the Lord. The day I rededicated my life to Christ, was the day I made a vow – '*no matter what comes my way, I will love you forever.*' The lyrics and music of the song came to me the day my husband led me back Christ right there in our living room.

I began to get inspiration to write my own songs, and in all my many years of ministry, this had never happened.

The songs began to minister to my heart. I started feeling better, my confidence returned, and God began to perfect His healing in my life.

The album, *The Encounter*, had a total of fifteen songs, and it was birthed in the place of healing, prayer and worship, encapsulating my walk with God.

Evans

2016. London, UK.

Our healing started in the place of our passion, our music ministry.

During this period of trials, we started to get a lot of invites for ministration which we honoured and showed up at.

My wife and I started to throw ourselves into work and ministry and every time Purist ministered, we felt the heavens open.

Purist received songs during these trying times. Unction began to grow. She would wake up with songs she had heard in her dream and she would record them on her phone and continue to develop them. The culmination of these songs formed *The Encounter.*

Clearly, these songs were deep songs inspired by heaven.

This kept us busy for a while as we worked to produce and launch the album.

Slowly, God was working out our healing.

Contrary to what we had expected, we didn't have to deal with pressures from our families. And we are so grateful for that miracle.

We had super-supportive family members who were sensitive enough to be there for us when we needed them without adding to our predicament. They prayed for us, constantly checked in on us but never pressured us.

We also had friends that were highly supportive, and a constant source of encouragement.

Our faith began to grow again, our service to God improved even more, our prayer life received more fire and gradually Purist stopped raising her brows at some of the prayer points I raised during devotions.

We were back on our feet – Purist started to pray much more, her faith grew and so did mine.

We began to encounter men of God who had also gone through challenges bearing their children, and through them, we received prophetic words that strengthened our faith.

Finally, this period of pain and struggle was coming to an end.

And we were more than thankful.

Section Four:

Kairos
2017 - 2018

22

Purist

2017. London, UK.

I woke up with a headache.

The previous night we had been at a concert, and it had been so energetic, the presence of God had been so strong. I thought about it and I smiled to myself.

My head throbbed again. It had to be another cold. I was always prone to having hay fever, so I thought it was another fever.

The thought of going to grab some drugs from the pharmacy came to me, and as I turned to Evans to tell him, another thought crossed my mind.

You could be pregnant.

Pregnant? Where had the thought sprung from? It had been two years since I had even been pregnant. And frankly, I had not been thinking about it. I had handed everything over to God.

On the day I rededicated my heart to God, I decided that if God wanted to make me a mother, He would. I had made a vow that day that whether or not I had children, I would serve Him, and never doubt Him, His will, His way, or His purpose. That was all that really mattered.

Go and do a pregnancy test.

As much as I tried, I couldn't shake the feeling, so I went to dig out the pregnancy test strips I had bought several months ago. As I searched in all the likely places, I spoke to myself, *Taking a test wouldn't really hurt. The results would be ready in no time, and I could move on and continue with my life.*

Five minutes later, I had done the test and examined the test strip for the result.

I saw two clear and distinct lines.

It was positive.

Aaaarg!!!

My head went blank.

I went straight to the room where Evans still slept, and I woke him up in a haze. "Babe I don't understand, what's this?"

He turned sleepy eyes towards me, "What's the matter, babe?" He asked.

I showed him the test strip, and he sat up immediately.

We looked at each other.

"Are you for real?"

For a moment, we were speechless, but we both had the same thoughts. Confusion ran through our minds. For the past couple of months, we had enjoyed relative peace, and the thought of going back to the madness was scary. We were not sure if we wanted to go back to the place we had been not too long ago.

Do we want to go through this again? Are we ready for this?

"How are you feeling?" I could see Evans looking at me with some form of uncertainty. "Are you okay?"

"I'm fine," I told him. "I feel perfectly fine."

"Just sit down," he began. "Don't go anywhere, this time, you just need to rest."

I could sense the agitation in his voice. The news of being pregnant that had once brought so much joy was making us filled with worry and trepidation.

My head was spiralling with the thoughts of what had happened in the last four pregnancies. *Lord, I don't know if I can go through all that again...*

I suddenly heard a voice in my spirit. The first time I had ever heard this voice was on the day I met Evans. It was the same voice that had said Evans was my husband.

This one is different.

"I just heard something," I said quietly to Evans. "I just heard in my spirit that this one is different."

This was a word I had received from God. I thought of what happened during the past pregnancies, and a shudder passed down my spine. I had a word from God, I was holding unto it.

Was it going to be enough?

Evans

2017. London, UK.

It had been an interesting night.

Purist and I had just gotten home after an amazing ministration where we praised God like never before, at a program where Pastor Matthew Ashimolowo had ministered and we were both exhausted. We had sang and worshipped our hearts out, and led hundreds of worshippers to the throne room of God.

The morning after, I was awakened from sleep by an agitated Purist. She was holding a pregnancy test strip, and the first thought that popped in my head was: 'where did *she find the boldness to do a pregnancy test?'*

It had been two years since our fourth miscarriage, and since then, there had been no sign of another pregnancy. And there had been some relative peace in our lives.

With the pregnancy, fear tried to creep into my mind but I rebuked it, and didn't give it a foothold.

After we had assimilated the shock of the discovery, we went straight to the hospital. The doctors recommended that because of our history of miscarriages, Purist be placed on Aspirin for the duration of this pregnancy. With our shaky faith, we refused, and insisted that if our faith had brought us this far, it was sufficient to take us all the way. So we said No to Aspirin. We truly believed that this one was going to be sustained by God and so we didn't need Aspirin.

The doctors also recommended that Purist put a cerclage in place, a procedure that had to do with tying the cervix, to prevent a miscarriage from occurring. We refuted, and told the doctors that this was God's work, He had started it, and we were confident that He would finish it.

And all through the pregnancy, we had no issues.

Every now and then Purist would panic because she couldn't feel the baby moving and we'd rush to the hospital only to find out everything was fine.

We took communion every day, prayed, and had our pastors, parent and friends pray with us as well.

Purist

2017. London, UK.

From the moment I found out I was pregnant, everything about my life changed. For starters, Evans who manages me, cancelled all my singing engagements, and I stopped going out till I was about five months pregnant. I was placed on bed rest for up to twenty-five weeks – no shopping, no outings – nothing. I was home in the care of my husband who cooked, clean and took care of me. I was doing everything I could from home, and I tried to take things as easy as I possibly could.

The pregnancy was a smooth one, it was strange because it was different from all the earlier experiences – there was no bleeding, no ambulance trips, and no health issues, whatsoever.

Along the way, a second ovarian cyst was discovered in my right ovary, but by the grace of God, it dried up, my blood vessels worked perfectly, it was a perfectly healthy pregnancy.

I was always afraid that something was going to happen, but day in and day out, the pregnancy progressed with such ease, it was unbelievable - this one was different!

Evans

2017. London, UK.

We believed that we would have a boy because years before, we had received a name for our baby. God dropped the name of our son into our spirit, five years before He dropped him into our arms.

We had been at a program where Rev. Funke Felix-Adejumo was ministering in London when she mentioned the name *Kairos* and gave the meaning as *The Lord's Appointed Time.* The moment she said *Kairos*, it dropped in my spirit – that was going to be the name of our child, and my wife got the same exact word, at the same time!

Two years after, we were at a church program for expectant parents and the Pastor gave a word. He said God had given a couple a name for their unborn child, and that name was an indication of what He planned to do in their lives.

I immediately sensed that the word the Pastor had received was specifically for us, and I told Purist as soon I got the chance. It was later confirmed by the Pastor that the word was indeed ours!

Purist

2017. London, UK.

When I was about 20 weeks pregnant, we went for a scan. We had received the name *Kairos* five years ago, and we were trusting God for a boy.

The doctors checked the baby's heart, lungs, and they said everything was fine.

After all the major checks had been done, and everything was verified to be in perfect condition, the technician suddenly asked, "Do you want to know what the sex of the baby is?"

We had looked at each other excitedly. In all our other pregnancies, we had never come this far as having the option to find out if it had been a boy or a girl. It was a thrilling time for us!

The technician looked back at the screen. "I can see the area clearly," he said, with a warm disposition. "You are expecting a boy."

That was amazing news!

Evans was all over the place, he couldn't contain himself. I don't think I had ever seen him that excited.

As he drove back from the hospital, I noticed that he was driving very slowly, and it occurred to me that he was extra careful so he didn't jolt the baby!

It was the best news ever!

It only confirmed for us that our baby Kairos was finally on the way.

23

Purist

2018. London, UK.

Every morning, I woke up with apprehension and a fear that something could go wrong with the baby. My previous experiences made me jittery, and each time I saw a slight stain, or anything familiar that reminded me of the past, and I would suddenly begin to worry.

I only started enjoying my period of pregnancy when I was about seven months gone, because I believed that at this point, the pregnancy would stay.

God had given me a word. He had spoken to my heart and said this one was different, but I still wrestled with fear and doubt, and I struggled inwardly every day.

What if something went wrong?

What if after everything, we ended up exactly where we started…

What if… just what if?

When my faith level was low, I would call my mum in tears, and she would encourage me with kind, positive words.

The fear of what I had gone through, and the fear of having to go through anything like that again was a heavy weight to bear, and it was emotionally draining.

I shared my struggles with a friend of mine, and she said God had dropped in her spirit that we should pray and ask God for mercy.

Lord, please have mercy….

I started praying to the God of mercy.

I knew I had been having doubts, and I also knew that God made the children of Israelites go through the wilderness because of their unbelief. I knew that God hated unbelief, and when we operated in that realm, it was hurtful. I was trying – I believed God, but beneath it all, there was still a nudge of fear…

Lord, have mercy! Lord, I believe… but help my unbelief!

I prayed fervently that day, "I believe, but help my unbelief. Lord, I have been through hell, and all that can see me through is your grace."

As I was saying this prayer, I fell asleep.

As I slept, a song stirred within my spirit.

Chi debere ...

I woke up, with a gentle assurance that God had spoken a word in my spirit - *Chi debere. Chi debere* literally meant God is merciful.

It was a confirmation of God's word to me.

Initially, I was confused, I thought God should have given me a song that said *I'm here with you,* or something like *don't worry... it is well with your soul.*

Instead, He gave me a song proclaiming His mercy.

When I thought about it, I realised God was saying to me that celebration was assured because he'd had mercy on me and there was no need for me to fret. He had taken care of everything, all the way to celebration. The Lord had gone into the future, and He was assuring me that all was well with this pregnancy.

His song was not just for the period of the pregnancy, it was a song for celebration after the baby had been born!

Glory to God!

Just like the other song the Lord had given me two years earlier – *Idiri-mu-ma,* which literally meant *God has done me well.* It did not make sense then, because I had gone through so much pain. But when God had given me that song, He had given me the song for the future. He was talking about my being pregnant.

It suddenly made so much sense.

I held unto that word from God and night and day. *Chi debere*, and I wrote the lyrics and the music for the song:

If you hear my story

How he turned my life around

A laughing stock but He had

A perfect plan to light up my world

Exceedingly and abundantly above

He has done for me

He's turned my mourning to dancing

Put a song of praise in my mouth

{Chorus}

Chidebere

Omekwalam Ozor

I began to sing that song for the remainder of the pregnancy. I hummed the tune at every chance I got – my faith was building, my peace was restored – I stopped fretting and worrying, and I began to celebrate!

24

Purist

2018. London, UK.

The date was 27th of March.

I had passed my due date by five days.

Five whole days.

It was the longest time I've had to wait. I had done everything the doctors had said I should do. Daily, I did as much exercise as I could – I climbed the stairs, I walked around – I was ready for this baby to come! Why wasn't the baby coming?

My mind was a compendium of thoughts. *Why is the baby staying longer than necessary? Is there a reason to worry?*

A lot of thoughts swept through my mind.

Should I opt for a caesarean section? Is it still safe for the baby to be in the womb for so long?

Lord, have mercy!

We went to the hospital, and the doctors took my weight, checked the baby and said everything was fine. "Some babies chose to stay in the womb longer than others," they said, "and you don't need to worry, it's perfectly normal."

The baby's head was already down, and I was feeling a lot of pressure, but labour had not yet kicked in. The doctors performed a sweep to get the labour started, and they sent me back home to wait for the baby.

The tension was mounting, and I couldn't wait to meet our little man.

Evans

2018. London, UK.

It was a few days after forty weeks and the baby was not coming.

Purist was getting worried, wondering why the baby hadn't come, and I did all I could to allay her fears as I reassured her that everything was fine. We had prayed, it had been a stress-free pregnancy, God was in control!

We had both gone to the mall that day to buy a few things. I still remember that it was a cool and brilliant evening. Shortly after we walked into the mall, she froze in her tracks, grabbed me by the hand, and with a dead-serious expression, she said, '*Babes, I think my water has broken!*'

The shock. It was sudden. We had been expecting this for so long; we just couldn't believe it was finally happening.

We jumped into the car, sped back home, grabbed her already packed bag, and headed straight for the hospital.

Purist

2018. London, UK

I went to the mall with my hubby because it was an opportunity to walk around and do anything I could to get the labour process going.

I suddenly started feeling very wet, I started having contractions, and the next thing, a big gush of water, followed by an intense pain I would never forget.

People were looking at me as I bent over, groaning in pain. Evans went to get the car, and a security guard supported me while I waited for him to get back with the car. At that time, it was about after eight in the evening, and the contractions were coming every six minutes.

Before then, I had placed a call to my Pastor in my very worried state, laying my concerns of our baby being late, right then she spoke prophetically that in forty eight hours our baby would be born and delivered by Pastor Folake, a pastor in one of the RCCG branches who was a midwife at the *Balsidon University Hospital*, where I was to have the baby. The odds of that happening were slim, but we prayed and believed that it would happen as we had declared.

When we called the hospital to inform them that I had gone into labour, Pastor Folake responded. God had answered our prayers – she was on duty that night!

She asked us to come to the hospital right away, and she had prepared a room for me. Pastor Folake ensured that I had been assigned the best floor, and I got a room to myself.

We got to the hospital by about 9pm. At that time, I was about 3cm dilated. I remained 3cm dilated for a long time, and the midwives were concerned because usually a woman had to be 10cm dilated for a birthing to occur.

Nothing was happening, and the baby was being monitored, to be sure everything was progressing normally.

I had this strong conviction to worship, and I told Evans. I had compiled a playlist of a few of our songs that we had done in the past, and as it played in the background, we worshipped along with it for two hours non-stop.

You are bigger than what people say…

Jesus, you love me too much ooo…

The presence of God was so strong in that room, I could feel Him move, I could feel a reassurance that everything would turn out well. The songs went into my spirit, and gave me a reaffirmation that I was not alone – God was with me, and by His grace and power, together we would birth this glorious miracle.

By the time the nurses came to check me, I had moved from 3cm dilated to 9cm. it was a big jump, they couldn't even get over it!

And the next thing, they prepared me – the baby was coming!

"I can see the head!" One of the midwives started.

"Don't push yet, don't push yet…." Another midwife said, and then finally, I heard, "Okay, push…"

And I pushed for like six or seven times

And the baby was out…

Evans

2018. London, UK

I watched my wife as she laboured, she was in a lot of pain, three centimetres dilated and screaming in anguish. Apparently, she had quite some distance to go before the baby could be born.

At that point I wished I could help bear some of the pain she was going through. She was given painkillers and I just stood there unable to think, she then asked me to play some worship songs as we both started to worship.

Immediately the atmosphere there and then changed as she told me what songs to play and eventually drifted off to sleep, which worried her mum because she wasn't supposed to be sleeping during labour.

The midwives came to check about two hours later and found her to be nine centimetres dilated, shockingly. At that time, she was ready to push and I went to a corner to pray because I couldn't watch.

I turned around after some minutes and I saw our baby's head, the midwives cheered; Purist was doing a great job!

Few minutes later, at the appointed time, which was 7am, 28th of March, 2018, our baby was in Purist's arms.

He had finally arrived!

I took pictures and filmed as I watched my wife weep at God's faithfulness.

25

Purist

2018. London, UK.

I heard the sound of his cry.

Goose bumps suddenly appeared all over me. It was a feeling I don't think I would ever be able to accurately describe.

He's alive!

When they brought him and gave him to me, I burst into tears, held him tenderly in my arms, as he peered at me. His skin was smooth, soft, and so delicate. I was so tired, but I couldn't just let go.

It was like a dream come true. It was unbelievable.

I had waited for him all this while, and here he was in my arms, like he had always been there.

Someone wake me up! Am I dreaming?

Lord, this can only have been your doing...

Tears fell from my eyes.

CHI DEBERE... IDIRI MU MA... Lord, you have done me well!

This was the best feeling I had ever had.

Evans

2018. London, UK.

The day before our baby came, I had said that immediately I saw Kairos, I would shout so loudly, the entire hospital would hear.

As it turned out, the moment I saw Kairos, I had no strength to shout, all I could do was go on my knees and whisper '*Thank You Jesus.*'

After Purist had the baby, I called my mum, and told her the good news, and she just started screaming – '*Praise God!*' at the other end of the phone. I called my pastors, friends and joyously began sharing the good news.

The doctors released us to go home about mid-day that day but Purist decided she wanted to rest in the hospital for a while, and so my mother-in-law and I went home to freshen up, hoping Purist would get some sleep before we returned.

We got back at about 4 pm and she still hadn't slept. The joy and excitement of having Kairos had kept her awake!

I was reminded of the scripture that says '*When the Lord turned around the captivity of Zion, they were like them that dreamed.*' It felt like I was in a dream, almost the same way I felt on my wedding day. I was there but it felt like I wasn't there.

I looked at the child, *my* child and he looked at me, smiling and full of joy.

Everything was perfect. He was clean, fresh and without blemish. No complications at all.

Perfect, just like the Lord had said – in His own Time.

26

Evans

2018. London, UK.

It has been just a few months but parenting has been an amazing experience, so far!

My best times are when I am carrying Kairos and dancing and singing and laughing with so much joy. Just seeing and holding the manifestation of God's word and seeing how handsome he is, leaves me smiling from ear to ear, and then Purist has to whip out her phone and make a recording of this super-excited father!

It has been such an amazing experience that has made God become more real to me; a lot more than He has ever been.

Purist

2018. London, UK.

I wouldn't trade parenthood for anything in the world.

I wouldn't trade the cry of my baby for anything.

Anytime I see Kairos, I just want to hug him tightly, and every time I see him, I always say – *thank you Jesus!*

I am so thankful.

He poops on me, and I'm filled with joy… when he cries, I'm there by his side. He makes the slightest noise, and I'm picking him up, rocking him, or petting him – I can't get enough of him!

Thank you, Jesus!

Evans

2018. London, UK.

Every time I look at Kairos, I think – *wow!*

I carry him and I'm in awe of how a life, a healthy child came out of Purist's womb. It's unexplainable.

Carrying my son, looking at him reminds me of God's faithfulness, and of God's love. Kairos will forever be a reminder that there's a God and much more, there's a God that loves us.

I will never stop thanking God, and I will never get tired of praising Him on the account of this miracle of a child. I will never be ungrateful.

When Kairos comes of age, he will hear this story, read this book, and he will live out his purpose. He has come as a glory to God, and I believe Kairos is a prophecy, a strength to our family, and a strength to his nation.

Kairos has taught us that at the appointed time, God makes all things beautiful.

27

Evans & Purist

For Friends & Family of Waiting Parents

For the first time, many people would be hearing about some of our personal experiences, and they would marvel at the depth of some of the things we have been through. We have never publicly spoken about these things, except to our spiritual parents and close friends; only very few people knew the details of our struggles.

As we journeyed through our process, waiting for the manifestation of Kairos, one of the greatest strengths we had were the people around us – those who encouraged, prayed and stood in the gap over the years, and spiritually birthed and midwifed our amazing miracle. On the flip side, one of the greatest battles we faced were the people around us – those who didn't know how to behave or respond to us, and ignorantly made the pain much worse.

It's tough to wait for anything, and sometimes it's tougher to watch people you love, wait – there is always an irresistible urge to jump in, and fix the situation, the best way you know how. It's one of those difficult life moments where you struggle to say the right things, and do the right things, just to make things turn out perfectly. Sadly, some people in a bid to help waiting couples, have ignorantly ended up doing more harm than good.

Just like us, Waiting Parents have a lot of things they might not share – they might not talk much about their struggles, their pressures, how they stay awake at night, battle with insecurities, or the countless tears they shed. For this reason, please be sensitive!

Don't be quick to throw words at them, without carefully considering the effect of what you say. You just never know what they might have gone through, or what they might be currently going through – your words could be the healing balm they need for that season, or could lacerate and aggravate an already scalding and bleeding heart.

Sometimes, not talking about a problem is a greater way to show you care. If you must speak, learn to say the right words, or not say anything at all.

Waiting Couples should be seen first as individuals, as people, not as problems to be fixed; don't stigmatize them, and hound them with questions such as: "when are you going to have your children? What are you waiting for?"

No one desires to be in a situation where you desire to have something – a job, a spouse, a career change, a house, a child – you have done everything you possibly can to get it, and it's just not coming. Remember that God is the custodian of time, and He orchestrates and rules as He pleases.

As you tarry spiritually and emotionally with them through this process, the Lord will reward you, and in God's appointed time, you will have multiple reasons to celebrate with them!

For Waiting Parents

Our journey taught us to trust God, and to trust in His decree that we should be fruitful and multiply. We believed His word and gathered every scripture in the bible that talked about child bearing, fruitfulness and children generally.

For every parent in the bible that had to wait to have children – Hannah, Rebecca, Elizabeth, Abraham, these children were unique children, and they ended up being preferred to their peers. These parents were special, God reserved their blessings, and contrary to what they might have felt at some point in their lives, He hadn't forgotten them.

The devil only tries to lie to us. But it's best to believe that those children you have to wait for and pray for and believe for, are special children.

We would advise waiting parents to trust in the word of God. Gather relevant scriptures – pray it, speak it and believe it!

Throw yourself into God, into the service of God's kingdom. Make sacrifices, do things you have never done before. Let God know you and see your work, it's the best time to be closest to God and be active in spiritual things.

Don't believe the lie of the devil. From our experience, the devil will make you doubt everyone and everything including yourself, your salvation and everything you've ever believed. Renew your mind so often that it's hard to even hear the lies of the devil. The situation will make you want to say things that you'd regret after you see the manifestation, do not say them. Just like how Job was mocked and asked to curse God and die. Believe God despite all you see. Every month might seem as a roller coaster, but still believe God.

Forgive people and do not hold on to the insensitivity of people.

And most importantly, enjoy your life, live joyfully, and create the right environment for God to show up. Refuse to wallow in depression and self-pity, seek out your passion and anger the devil with it.

Do not lose the time just sitting and waiting for a miracle, Live instead!

Live until your miracle comes!

Don't let the experiences, the failures, or the challenges of the past prevent you from walking into the glorious destiny God has prepared for you.

Your miracle is around the corner.

Hold on!

Be strong!

Believe us when we say, indeed, it's worth the wait!

About Purist Ogboi

With a style that fuses contemporary rock, hip hop, neo-soul and ballad, **Purist Ogboi** can be best described as *strikingly different*. She is a breath of fresh air in the Gospel music scene with her strong dynamic vocals and endearing quirkiness.

Purist connects with the heart of the listener in a deep, stirring way, making her music impactful and unforgettable.

Purist is a graduate of BIMM "Tech Music Schools London" where she studied Vocals and

Music Performance.

In 2013 she released her debut EP titled I NEED YOU with 4 official videos. In August 28th, 2016, she released her 15 track album which she titled THE ENCOUNTER.

Her music has grown to be a blessing to many worldwide. In 2016, she was crowned **Premier Gospel's Best Newcomer** and **AGMMA** (African Gospel Music & Media Award) **Artiste of Excellence.**

She is married to the amazing, multi-award winning gospel music producer, Evans Ogboi, who gives soothing interpretation to her music, and they are blessed with a son.

For more about Purist, please visit *www.puristogboi.com*

About Evans Ogboi

Evans Ogboi is a multi award winning singer, songwriter, music producer, gospel recording artiste and motivational speaker.

He is a trained music producer and sound engineer from SAE London. Evans launched his record company, ***Simplicity Records*** in 2007 with the release of his debut album titled "Miracle." Since then he has produced countless records contributing massively to the body of kingdom music.

He's a ***BBC Songs of Praise***

finalist who also led the Living Faith Connections Choir to be the first choir to ever win UK's prestigious MOBO award Best Gospel ACT in 2014. His album titled "***Songs From My Heart***" was nominated best album premier ***Gospel Awards UK*** in 2016, and in 2018, he won the **Artiste of Excellence Europe** in the **AGMMA Awards.**

His music ministry remains a blessing to the body of Christ. With over 21 years of experience in church ministry, he is totally sold out to kingdom mandate.

Evans is married to Purist Ogboi, and they both serve in the music ministry and are blessed with a son.

For more about Evans Ogboi, please visit:
www.evansogboiministries.com

PURIST OGBOI
THE ENCOUNTER

AVAILABLE ON
www.evansogboiministries.com